Exploring English

Exploring English

A new intermediate course

Michael Thorn

ENGLISH LANGUAGE TEACHING

Prentice Hall

New York   London   Toronto   Sydney   Tokyo   Singapore

Published 1992 by
Prentice Hall International (UK) Limited
Campus 400
Maylands Avenue
Hemel Hempstead
Hertfordshire
HP2
A division of
Simon & Schuster International Group

First published by Cassell Publishers Limited 1979

Printed and bound in Great Britain by The Bath Press

British Library Cataloguing in Publication Data

Information available from the Publisher on request

ISBN 0-13-327727-5

Grateful acknowledgement for permission to use photographs
reproduced in this book is made to the following (numbers
refer to the pages in book on which they occur).

Barnaby's Picture Library (1, 6, 25, 28, 41, 45, 65, 91, 159);
British Airways (96); British Telecom (8); British Tourist
Authority (15, 33, 62, 74, 150, 161); Commissioner of Police
(81); Robert Genung (107); Jaguar Cars (86, 176); Michael
Leach/NHPA (23); Joy McKellen (68); Martin Mulloy
(123); National Gallery (59); Photo Source (39); Popperfoto
(94, 101, 113, 133, 142, 144); Swiss National Tourist Office
(73); Michael Thorn (11, 12, 48, 85).

Contents

To the teacher

Fashions change, not least in the world of teaching. Recently we have heard a great deal about Notional/Functional courses, and this "revolution" has made us all examine the ways we teach. The great advantage of the notional approach is that students can be taught to use the language for specific purposes, easily and quickly. Grammatically, "Would you like to come to the cinema this evening?" is a fairly complex item – more complex certainly than "Do you like films?" – but it might well be more useful, and thus we might wish to teach the more complex item first.

However, many students of English go on to take the First Certificate exam, the Proficiency, or even 'O' Level English, and these students need a sound grammatical base. This then is a grammar based course, into which I have tried to incorporate lessons learnt while using the notional approach. A student who completes this course will be ready to move straight on to a First Certificate Course.

Complicated grammar explanations don't help a student to speak or write a language accurately, but well chosen examples, thoroughly learnt, can help him towards that "feel" for the language, which is essential, if he is to speak and write naturally and well.

Language is necessary for people to express real thoughts, and students should be encouraged to express real ideas, wherever possible. It is more useful practice for a student to say "My landlady was making the breakfast when I came downstairs this morning" – undramatic, but something which really happened – than "The gangsters were coming out of the Bank when the Police arrived" – dramatic, but not related to the student's own experience. To learn to speak a language, it is necessary to *feel* the thoughts one is expressing.

For this reason each unit progresses from the text, in which the student will find "key" examples of the focal point, towards the "Ideas for Discussion" and "Composition", where the student will have the opportunity to give his opinion or talk about his own life.

I am most grateful to Joanna Gray for all her hard work and helpful advice. She has done a lot to improve the manuscript, but my mistakes remain my own.

Michael Thorn

To the student

Perhaps you will be in England when you use this book, or maybe you are studying English in your own country. As this is an Intermediate Course, you will certainly have been learning English for some time. So a lot of the things in the book will not be completely new for you. But when you are learning a language, you need to revise constantly, and the exercises are designed to help you to do this, and at the same time to learn new structures and vocabulary.

The people in the book are mostly the sort of people a student in England might come into contact with. They're not terribly rich, but they're not terribly poor either. They don't lead terribly exciting lives, but, on the whole, they enjoy themselves. They watch television, listen to the radio, work quite hard, go to football matches, wait in queues for buses, and complain about the weather and the tax man. Not all of them are English, for people of many nationalities live in England.

Each unit of the book has a focal point. There are two sections to each unit, an oral section, and a written section, and you will find exercises in the written section similar to those you have practised in the oral section. There is a text or conversation for each section of each unit, and you will find an example, or examples, of the focal point in each text. Having read, or listened to the text, you will do the practice exercises, finishing with a discussion topic, and, at the end of the written section, you will write a composition. The discussion topics and composition exercises are designed to help you to use the focal point in talking and writing about yourself, or about things I hope might interest you.

Many topics are touched on in the book: sport, a little history, social problems and so on. It's much easier to talk to English people if you know something about the things they are likely to be interested in.

If you want to learn to speak English, you should learn new words and structures in context. That means that it's much more useful to remember the example: "Oh, I've lost my ring", than it is to remember some complicated rule about when the Present Perfect tense is used.

You should keep a notebook and become a collector of thoughts, not words. Don't write too much on each page. Use coloured pencils to underline or put little boxes around new or important items. Remember too that you must learn how to say the things you write in your notebook. For instance the word "can't" isn't pronounced like "can" with a "t" on the end; it rhymes with "aunt".

Learning to speak a foreign language is hard work. But it's not quite so hard if you really *want* to learn, and are enjoying your lessons. I hope you will enjoy using this book.

Note for the fourth printing:

Thanks to the many teachers who have been kind enough to write to me with their comments, I have made some changes which will, I hope, improve the book. Those which may cause confusion are:

p.16 Change in verb table
p.20–21 Changes in dates on Curriculum Vitae and in Exercise B p.21
p.34 Change to Exercise B No.4
p.97 Change to Exercise B No.5

The corresponding changes will be made in the revised and enlarged Teacher's Book when it is available.

Old Arthur

Everyone knows him as Old Arthur. He lives in a little hut in the middle of a small wood, about a mile from the village. He visits the village store twice a week to buy food and paraffin, and occasionally he collects letters and his pension from the post office. A few weeks ago, a reporter from the local
5 newspaper interviewed him. This is what he said:

I get up every morning with the birds. There is a stream near my hut and I fetch water from there. It's good, clear, fresh water, better than you get in the city. Occasionally, in the winter, I have to break the ice. I cook simple food on my old paraffin stove; mostly stews and
10 things like that. Sometimes I go to the pub and have a drink, but I don't see many people. I don't feel lonely. I know this wood very well, you see. I know all the little birds and animals that live here and they know me. I don't have much money, but I don't need much. I think I'm a lucky man.

A   Oral questions

1 Where does Old Arthur live?
2 Who interviewed him recently?
3 How far is it to the village?
4 How often does Arthur go into the village?
5 What does he buy from the village store? (two things)
6 What does he collect from the post office? (two things)
7 Where does he get his water from?
8 What does he say about the water in the stream?
9 What sort of thing does Arthur cook?
10 What does he cook on?

B   Note these questions and answers:

Is he married?
No, he isn't.

Is he quite poor?
Yes, he is.

Does he have a job?
No, he doesn't.

Does he sometimes go to the pub?
Yes, he does.

Give short answers to the following questions:

1   Is Arthur quite old?
2   Is he a lonely man?
3   Is the store in the village?
4   Is the water in the stream clean?
5   Does Old Arthur see many people?
6   Does he get his water from a tap?
7   Does he like the birds and animals in the wood?
8   Does the stream sometimes freeze in winter?
9   Does Arthur cook on an electric stove?
10   Does he get his pension from the post office?

C   Imagine that you are interviewing old Arthur. These are the answers he gives to your questions. What were the questions you asked him?

1   In a little hut in the wood.
2   At the village store.
3   On my old paraffin stove.
4   Yes, I go there occasionally for a drink.
5   From the stream.
6   No, I never feel lonely.
7   Not much, my eyes aren't too good.
8   No, I haven't got a radio.
9   No, I was an only child, and my parents died when I was quite young.
10   No, I don't believe in doctors

D   Note this pattern:

He only sees a few people.
not/many people
HE DOESN'T SEE MANY PEOPLE

Make up more negative statements:

1   He only visits the village store twice a week.
not/every day
2   He only breaks the ice on the water occasionally.
not/often
3   He only collects his letters from the post office once a month.
not/every week
4   He cooks on a paraffin stove.
not/a gas stove
5   He lives in a hut in the wood.
not/an ordinary house
6   He gets his water from the stream.
not/a tap
7   There is no television in his hut.
not/television
8   There is no radio in his hut.
not/radio
9   He usually feels quite cheerful.
not/miserable
10   He only has one cooking pot.
not/complicated meals

E   Read the story about Peter and then answer the questions

Peter is a young officer in the bomb disposal squad. He is at present examining a suspicious parcel in a carrier bag in a big store.

He has a microphone round his neck, and he is reporting exactly what he is doing to his Commanding Officer:

"I am now approaching the carrier bag, and I can hear a ticking sound. I am now looking into the carrier bag. There are three parcels here. I am removing the first now. It is wrapped in white paper. It feels soft. I am unwrapping it now. It's a piece of fish.

"Here's something else. This is wrapped in brown paper. It's also soft. I am unwrapping it now. It's a green jumper.

"Now here's a square box. It could be an ordinary alarm clock, it could be a bomb. It's ticking. The box is wrapped in blue paper. I am unwrapping it now. Inside there's a green box with 'Smith's Clocks' printed on the lid. I can't see any wires. I'm taking off the lid now. . . . It's an alarm clock. It's a blue Smith's alarm clock.'

1   Who does Peter work for?
2   What is he doing at the moment?
3   What has he got round his neck?
4   What can Peter hear coming from the carrier bag?
5   What are the two things that might be in there?
6   What is the first parcel wrapped in?
7   What is in this parcel?
8   What is in the brown parcel?
9   What is printed on the lid of the green box?
10   What is in the parcel?

F   George and Helen are in different rooms.

HELEN   What are you doing?
GEORGE   I'm just writing a note to Frank.

Make up some more conversations:

1   make/coffee
2   look through/slides
3   tidy/kitchen
4   mend/this plug
5   look for/stamp
6   put new batteries/radio
7   press/trousers
8   take film/out of the camera
9   get/sandwich
10   wind/clock

G   Imagine you bump into[1] an old friend you haven't seen for some time. You ask him various questions.

You want to know how he is getting on.
You say: How are you getting on?

Make up some more questions:

1   You want to know if he is enjoying life.
2   You want to know where he is living now.
3   You want to know if he is still sharing a flat with his friend Paul.
4   You want to know if he is still working at the same place.
5   You want to know if he is still working very hard.
6   You want to know if he is still going out with Anna.
7   You want to know if he is still doing the football pools.
8   You want to know if he is still driving that old Morris.

H   Idea for discussion

Play the old television game, What's My Line?

One student pretends he is a waiter, a nurse, a bank clerk, etc., and everyone else asks questions to try and find out what the job is.

Do you work outside? Do you earn a big salary? Do you work in an office?

If you ask twenty questions without guessing what the job is, the student has beaten the class.

Note how we form the SIMPLE PRESENT

		make	
STATEMENTS	I You	make	a lot of noise.
	He/she/it	makes	
	We You They	make	

[1] bump into: to meet unexpectedly

UNIT 1   Simple Present/Present Continuous

NEGATIVES	I You	*don't	make	a lot of noise.
* Contractions for *do not* and *does not*, normally used in spoken English.	He/she/it	*doesn't		
	We You They	*don't		

QUESTIONS	Do	I you	make	a lot of noise?
	Does	he/she/it		
	Do	we you they		

Note how we form the PRESENT CONTINUOUS

STATEMENTS	I	am	working.
Note: We often use I'M WORKING, HE'S WORKING, etc. in spoken English.	You	are	
	He/she/it	is	
	We You They	are	

NEGATIVES	I	am	not working.
Note: We often use I'M NOT WORKING, HE'S NOT WORKING, etc. in spoken English.	You	are	
	He/she/it	is	
	We You They	are	

QUESTIONS	Am	I	working?
	Are	you	
	Is	he/she/it	
	Are	we you they	

4

Special points to note

When you have mastered the **simple present tense**, you will be able to talk about things that:

a) happen regularly (or never)
b) are (or aren't) always true.

Examples:

WHERE DOES THE QUEEN LIVE?

SHE LIVES AT BUCKINGHAM PALACE.
I DON'T BELIEVE POLITICIANS ARE ALWAYS COMPLETELY HONEST.

WE HAVE BREAKFAST AT EIGHT O'CLOCK.

You'll find that you often use the **simple present** together with adverbs of time like this:

I OFTEN GO FOR A SWIM IN THE MORNING.

OLD ARTHUR SOMETIMES GOES TO THE PUB.

IT NEVER SNOWS IN SUMMER.

Note the short form of reply which is frequently used:

Do you like it here?
Yes, I do. *or* No, I don't.

Does she like it here?
Yes, she does. *or* No, she doesn't.

Is this Bedford Square?
Yes, it is. *or* No, it isn't.

Are you Mr Hapsburg?
Yes, I am. *or* No, I'm not.

Special points to note

You will need the **present continuous** to describe an action that is or isn't happening at the moment the speaker is speaking.

Examples:

HELP! HELP! I'M DROWNING.

THIS TYPEWRITER ISN'T WORKING PROPERLY.

HE'S CATCHING HIM. (COMMENT ON A RACE)

Problem:

The **present continuous** is often confused with the **simple present**, but the distinction is really quite clear.

Compare these ideas:

I'm helping with the washing-up (*at the moment*)
I always (*usually, often*) help with the washing-up

I'm in the kitchen . . . I'm watching television
I often watch television in the kitchen

The **present continuous** form is also used to talk about future events. We shall examine this use in the next unit.

Albion Street

Albion Street is a small street near London Airport. It is eleven o'clock on a hot, summer Sunday morning.

At the end of Albion Street is the motorway, and as usual, there is a steady stream of traffic travelling to and from the airport. Big jets are
5 passing overhead at the rate of one every three or four minutes. But the people who live in Albion Street hardly notice. They are busy with their own lives.

Mr Curtis, the grocer, is cleaning his blue van, while on the other side of the road young Keith Smith is polishing his new sports car.
10 Mrs Pasolini, whose husband owns the fish and chip shop, is talking to the Jamaican lady who lives next door, and Mr Kapuscinski, the Polish tailor, is examining his roses, for signs of greenfly.

A contented community, you may think, but the inhabitants of Albion Street are worried, because the GLC[1] have plans for 'developing' the area.

A Questions

1 Where is Albion Street?
2 What is happening on the motorway?
3 What is happening in the sky above Albion Street?
4 Ask what Mr Curtis is doing.
5 Answer the question.
6 What is Keith Smith doing?
7 What does Mrs Pasolini's husband own?
8 Who is she talking to?
9 What is Mr Kapuscinski doing?
10 What does he do?
11 Ask why the inhabitants of Albion Street are worried.
12 Answer the question.

[1] GLC: Greater London Council (the City council for London)

B Look at this pattern:

Mr Curtis/clean van
Mr Curtis is cleaning his van.

Mrs Curtis/clean van
Mrs Curtis isn't cleaning the van.

Use the ideas below to make up some more sentences, describing what people are or aren't doing:

1 Mr Curtis/his van
2 Keith/polish sports car
3 Mrs Pasolini/work in the fish and chip shop
4 Jamaican lady/talk to Mr Kapuscinski
5 Mr Kapuscinski/look at roses
6 Jamaican lady/talk to Mrs Pasolini
7 Mr Kapuscinski/look for greenfly
8 Mr Curtis/work his garden
9 Mrs Pasolini/talk to Mr Curtis
10 Mrs Pasolini/feel worried

C Look at these patterns:

Ask if I like sugar in my coffee.
Do you like sugar in your coffee?

Ask if David likes sugar in his coffee.
Does David like sugar in his coffee?

Make up some more questions:

1 Ask if I speak Spanish.
2 Ask if I read a newspaper every day.
3 Ask if David reads a newspaper every day.
4 Ask if David sometimes plays tennis.
5 Ask if I ever play tennis.
6 Ask if I often go to the theatre.
7 Ask if David sometimes goes to the theatre.
8 Ask if I usually get up early.
9 Ask if David usually gets up early.
10 Ask if David sometimes goes to church.

D Look at these ideas:

A pilot . . .
A pilot flies an aeroplane

An artist . . .
An artist paints pictures

Complete the following sentences in the same way, using ideas of your own:

1 A postman . . .
2 A tailor . . .
3 A grocer . . .
4 A musician . . .
5 A secretary . . .
6 A taxi-driver . . .
7 A baker . . .
8 A jockey . . .

E Composition

Write a letter to a friend who doesn't speak your mother tongue. Tell your friend where you are, what you are doing, and what you do during the week.

UNIT 2　Simple Present or Present Continuous?
Present Continuous as a Future

Cathy and Steve

Cathy and Steve are engaged, but unfortunately Cathy lives in Sussex and
Steve in Yorkshire. It is nine o'clock on Saturday morning, when the
phone rings beside Steve's bed. He is still asleep.

STEVE　Hello?
5　CATHY　Hello dear, where are you?
　　STEVE　Where all civilised people should be at this time on a Saturday
　　　　morning – in bed.

CATHY Lazy thing!

STEVE What do you mean 'lazy thing'? I earn my rest. I work jolly hard,
10   you know.

CATHY Of course you do, dear.

STEVE What about you? What are you doing?

CATHY At the moment I'm drinking a cup of coffee and talking to my lazy
        fiancé, but later I'm going shopping. That's what I want to talk to
15   you about.

STEVE Mmm.

CATHY I'm getting the curtains for the bedroom.

STEVE Good.

CATHY Do you like the idea of pale green?

20 STEVE That sounds all right.

CATHY Plain . . . then there won't be any problem when we come to buy
        the carpet. But I want to order the curtains today, because Aunt
        Phyllis is staying, and she's giving us the curtains as a wedding
        present. So we're going together to choose the material.

25 STEVE That's a good idea.

CATHY And what are you doing today?

STEVE Well, this morning I've got a little shopping to do, then this
        afternoon I'm going to the football[1] with Jim.

CATHY All right, Love, enjoy yourself. Bye.

30 STEVE Same to you. Bye.

A Oral questions

1 Do Cathy and Steve see one another every day?
2 If not, why not?
3 Why isn't Steve at work when the phone rings?
4 What does Cathy call Steve?
5 How does he defend himself?
6 What is Cathy doing while she's talking to Steve?
7 What is she planning to buy?
8 Who is paying for them?
9 Is she planning to buy flowered material?
10 Where is Steve going this afternoon?

---

[1] the football (match)

UNIT 2   Simple Present or Present Continuous? Present Continuous as a Future

B   Do you remember Peter (in Unit 1)? This story is about him. Put the verbs enclosed in brackets into the correct tenses:

Peter (*work*) for the bomb disposal squad. When people (*find*) something that (*look*) like a bomb, the bomb disposal squad are called, and they have to find out if it (*be*) a bomb or not. Today is Monday. At the moment Peter (*not examine*) any strange parcels. He (*sit*) in his office and (*read*) a number of official letters and notices.

Whenever the bomb disposal squad (*find*) a new sort of bomb, they always (*send*) a full description of it to all the bomb disposal teams. So Peter always (*read*) his official letters very carefully and (*study*) any diagrams they may contain.

C   Sometimes we use the PRESENT CONTINUOUS tense to make a future statement. Look at this situation:

Fred is a bachelor and his life is very carefully organised. Brenda, one of the young secretaries in the office where Fred works, thinks he is rather nice. She suggests that they might go to a film together one evening.

"What about Monday evening?" she asks.

"Oh!" says Fred, "on Monday evening I'm taking my washing to the launderette."

Now you play the part of Fred. Answer Brenda's questions using the ideas below:

1   What about Tuesday evening?
    HAVE/SUPPER/SISTER

2   What about Wednesday evening?
    GO/MY EVENING CLASS

3   What about Thursday evening?
    PLAY/BADMINTON

4   What about Friday evening?
    MEET/HARRY/DRINK

5   What about Saturday evening?
    WATCH/FOOTBALL/TELEVISION

6   What about Sunday evening?
    GO/CHURCH

D   When Steve is talking to Cathy in the conversation at the beginning of this unit, he says:

. . . I'm going to the football with Jim.

Use the notes below to make up similar sentences, using the present continuous as a future.

1   I/see/Mr Allen/tomorrow
2   I/go/pictures/this evening
3   The President/come/London/next week
4   I/buy/some new shoes/at the weekend
5   He/change/his job/after Christmas
6   They/move/to the seaside/in the spring
7   We/go/to Spain/next month
8   They/open/a new store/on twentieth July
9   I/ask for a rise/at the end of the week
10 I/get/that record/Saturday

E   Cathy asks Steve this question:

What are you doing today?

Use the notes below to make up questions you might ask your friend.

1   Where/go/this afternoon
2   Why/go/into the city
3   Who/go/party with
4   What/do/tomorrow
5   Where/buy/shoes
6   When/go/dentist
7   When/get/tickets for the concert
8   Where/meet/Paul/this evening
9   What time/come/tomorrow
10 Why/come/so late

F   Idea for discussion

Look at some more examples of the present continuous used as a future:

I'M GETTING MARRIED NEXT MAY¡
(*Note:* The ring has been bought, the arrangements have been made, the invitations have been printed.)

I'M GOING TO THE FOOTBALL MATCH ON SATURDAY.
(*Note:* Either you know there will be no problem about getting in, or you already have your ticket.)

Simple Present or Present Continuous? Present Continuous as a Future

B Look at this picture of boats on a river and then put the verbs in the passage below into the correct tenses:

In Cambridge the students often (*take*) their girl friends for trips up and down the river in boats like this. We (*call*) them punts. The students (*steer*) them with a long pole. They also (*use*) the pole to propel the boat through the water. In a rowing boat, of course, you (*do*) this with oars.

The young man in the picture (*stand*) at the back of the punt. He (*do*) all the work while his two girl friends enjoy the sunshine. A little group of people (*stand*) on the bridge. They (*watch*) the boats passing underneath and I think the man standing by himself (*take*) a photograph.

Of course a great many foreigners (*visit*) Cambridge in the summer. I sometimes (*think*) it must make it rather difficult for the students to study.

C Look at these ideas:

When are you going to Germany?
I'm going on Friday.
John isn't coming.

Use the notes below to make up similar sentences:

1 What time/you/come/Saturday?
2 Who/come/party?
3 Tom and Sue/not/come
4 Is it true/Peter/change/job?
5 George/get/new car
6 Where/buy/it?
7 You/watch/horror movie/tonight?
8 Which channel/they/show/it on?
9 Mike/go/abroad
10 When/he/leave?

D Composition

You are the personal assistant to a very important man, who works at your embassy in London. It's Monday and you are going through his programme for the week with him. Here is an example of the entries you have made in his diary.

Monday	3.00pm	Mr. Steffen from German Embassy

You say: "At 3.00 pm you're seeing Mr Steffen from the German Embassy."

Below are the complete notes for one week. Look at them carefully, then write the conversation between you and your boss:

Monday	3.00pm.	Mr. Steffen from German Embassy.
	8.00pm.	Dinner at Claridges Hotel. Turkish Ambassador.
Tuesday	10.00am.	Meeting with our Ambassador.
	1.00pm.	Lunch, Post Office Tower. British Post Office officials.
Wednesday	10.00am.	Appointment at Board of Trade. Discuss new import duties.
	1.00pm.	Guest speaker at Rotary Club lunch. Subject 'links between our two countries'
Thursday	11.00am.	Visit to University of Kent.
	6.00pm.	Attend cocktail party at German Embassy.
Friday	9.35am.	Heathrow. Fly to Paris to visit Trade Fair.

13

On a London Bus

A strange thing happened to Henri yesterday. He was on a bus and wanted to get off. So he stood up and rang the bell. To make sure the driver heard him he rang it twice, but the bus didn't stop, and the conductor came and shouted at him.

5   The conductor was so annoyed, and spoke so fast, that Henri didn't understand a word. The bus stopped at the next bus stop and Henri got off. As he got off he heard someone say: "I think he's a foreigner."

    When Henri got home, he told his landlady about the incident.

    "How many times did you ring the bell?" she asked.

10   "Twice," said Henri.

    "Well, that's the signal for the driver to go on," his landlady explained. "Only the conductor is allowed to ring the bell twice. That's why he got so annoyed."

    Henri nodded. "I see," he said.

A Oral questions

1 Where was Henri?
2 What did he want to do?
3 How did Henri indicate to the driver that he wanted to get off?
4 How many times did he ring the bell?
5 Why did he ring it twice?
6 Did the bus stop?
7 What did it do?
8 What did the conductor do?
9 Why couldn't Henri understand the conductor?
10 Was the conductor annoyed?
11 What did Henri do when the bus stopped?
12 What did he hear someone say?
13 Who did he tell about the incident?
14 Who is allowed to ring the bell twice?
15 What did Henri do to show his landlady that he understood?

B **Note how we form the negative of the SIMPLE PAST:**

. . . the bus didn't stop . . .
. . . Henri didn't understand a word.

Use the ideas below to make up negative statements in the past:

1 Henri/ring bell/four times
2 Henri/try to open/door
3 The driver/shout at Henri
4 The conductor/smile at Henri
5 The conductor/speak very slowly
6 When Henri/home/tell his father/incident

C **Note this sentence:**

He wanted to get off.

Think of possible answers to the following questions beginning:

I wanted to . . .

1 Why did you go into that café?
2 Why did you take that book out of the library?
3 Why did you go into that telephone box?
4 Why did you go into that pub?
5 Why were you so annoyed that you couldn't get into the cinema?
6 Why were you so angry when you couldn't get tickets for the football match?
7 Why did you bring your camera?
8 Why were you so cross because there wasn't any hot water?
9 Why did you bring your tennis racket?
10 Why did you go to the supermarket?

UNIT 3 Simple Past

D Think about last Saturday. Can you remember six things you did, and six things you didn't do?

E Look at this conversation between Maria and her landlady, Mrs Robinson:

It is breakfast time in Mrs Robinson's home, where Maria is staying.

MARIA	Oh dear. I got home very late last night. I hope I didn't disturb you.
MRS ROBINSON	No, I didn't hear a thing.
MARIA	George and I went to the pictures and we missed the last train.
MRS ROBINSON	That was bad luck. What did you do?
MARIA	Well, we tried to find the all-night bus stop, but nobody could tell us where it was, so finally we took a taxi.
MRS ROBINSON	My goodness, that was expensive, wasn't it?
MARIA	Yes, he charged us £5.

Note how we ask questions in the **simple past:**

Did you enjoy the film?
Yes, we did. *or* No, we didn't.

Now do this exercise:

1 Ask if Mrs Robinson heard Maria come in.
2 Answer the question.
3 Ask if Maria came home late.
4 Answer the question.
5 Ask who Maria went to the pictures with.
6 Answer the question.
7 Ask how they came home.
8 Answer the question.
9 Ask why they didn't come home by bus.
10 Answer the question.
11 Ask how much the taxi driver charged them.
12 Answer the question.

F Idea for discussion

Losing things can be very annoying; a key perhaps, or theatre tickets. Think of something you lost. Did you find it again? Talk about the incident.

Note how we form the SIMPLE PAST:

STATEMENTS	I You etc.	missed	the train yesterday.	

NEGATIVES	I You etc.	didn't (did not)	miss	the train yesterday.

QUESTIONS	Did	I you etc.	miss	the train yesterday?

16

Many verbs add -**ed** to form the SIMPLE PAST:

A strange thing happen**ed** to Henri . . .

. . . his landlady explain**ed** . . .

However there are also many verbs that form their past by changing their spelling in other ways. You have already met:

to stand	He stood up.
to hear	The driver heard him.
to ring	He rang it twice.
to come	The conductor came.
to speak	He spoke so fast.

These just have to be learnt and it is a good idea to keep a list and learn them carefully as you meet them.

Special points to note

We use the SIMPLE PAST to talk about an action that took place at a definite point of time in the past.

Examples:

A STRANGE THING HAPPENED TO HENRI YESTERDAY.

DID YOU SEE THAT PROGRAMME ABOUT TELEPATHY LAST NIGHT?

YES, I DID or NO, I DIDN'T.

Very often the point of time is understood rather than actually stated in the sentence. Look at this example:

"YESTERDAY WE WENT TO WINDSOR."

"DID YOU SEE ANY OF THE ROYAL FAMILY?"

"NO, BUT WE HAD A VERY INTERESTING DAY."

The YESTERDAY in the first sentence establishes the time so that all the other verbs used in the conversation are in the simple past as well, and all the statements refer to what happened (or did not happen) yesterday.

Here are some more typical points of time in the past:

last week/last night/on Tuesday/in 1964

There is also the expression AGO. We shall practise using this in the next unit.

WRITTEN SECTION

A Customer Pays his Bill

Last week the manager of an old-established[1] jeweller's shop received a letter marked 'personal', so of course his secretary gave it to him unopened. As he was very busy, the letter lay on his desk till tea-time. Then he opened it and a £10 note fell out onto his desk. With the note was
5   a short letter. This is what it said:

Dear Sir,

In 1935 I got engaged. But unfortunately at that time there was a lot of unemployment and I lost my job. I was six months without a job and then I got work again, but of course I was very short of money.

---

[1] old-established: it has been there a long time

10   I came to your shop to buy a wedding ring. The assistant brought some rings for me to look at, but she was called away for a moment, and I put one of the rings in my pocket. When she came back, I said I did not know the size of my girl-friend's finger. So I left the shop without buying a ring.

15   My wife died a short while ago and the fact that I never paid for her ring has been on my conscience all these years. At the time the ring cost £2, so I reckon that is about £10 at today's prices, and I am sending you that amount.

Yours truly,

A customer.

"Well, well, well," said the manager, "life is full of surprises!"

A Write short answers to the following questions:

1 What sort of shop is this story about?
2 Who received the letter?
3 Why didn't his secretary open it?
4 What fell out of the letter?
5 What happened to the writer of the letter in 1935?
6 What was there a lot of at this time?
7 What happened to the man's wife a short time ago?
8 What fact has been on the writer's conscience for many years?

B Now write some questions about the story and answer them, using as few words as possible.

1 Ask what the manager received.
2 Ask where it lay till tea-time.
3 Ask what the letter contained.
4 Ask what the writer lost in 1935.
5 Ask why the customer came to the shop.
6 Ask why the assistant left him alone with the rings.
7 Ask where the customer put one of the rings.
8 Ask what the customer said about his girl-friend's finger.
9 Ask what the ring cost in 1935.
10 Ask what the manager said, after reading the letter.

C Now write ten sentences about yourself. Mention:

1 Someone you met yesterday.
2 A place you visited last year.
3 The name of the last film you saw, and where you saw it.
4 An interesting programme you watched on the television, and when you watched it.
5 Where you spent last Christmas.
6 How you slept last night.
7 What you had for breakfast this morning.
8 What you had for dinner yesterday.
9 Somewhere you didn't go last week.
10 Somebody you didn't see yesterday.

Composition

You are a detective. In your area there is a firm specialising in crash repairs. The police are suspicious. They believe this firm may be handling stolen cars. You are given the job of watching their yard, and reporting on everything that happens.

You have a cassette recorder with you. This is what you put on your tape this morning:

8.00 a.m.	4th October. I took up my position ten minutes ago. Rather a cold morning.
8.15 a.m.	A blue Cortina is pulling up. A short, dark man with a big moustache is getting out. He's opening the gates to the yard.
8.35 a.m.	An orange Datsun is stopping. A tall, thin man is getting out. He's gone into the yard too.
9.15 a.m.	The dark man is driving out of the yard in an old, green breakdown truck.
10.10 a.m.	The breakdown truck is returning. It's towing a green Fiat. The front of the Fiat is badly damaged.
11.15 a.m.	Two West Indians have just driven up in a red Cortina. The side is damaged. The dark man is coming out. He's looking at the damage. They're discussing it. They're leaving it and walking off.
12.10 p.m.	A very old grey van has stopped. The driver is a small man, wearing an old blue pullover and jeans. He's gone into the yard. Now he's coming out with the dark man. They're looking at the rust on the side of the van. The dark man is examining it. He's shaking his head. The little man is getting in the van again. He's driving off.
12.30 p.m.	The tall man and the dark man are coming out. The dark man is locking the gates. Both men are getting into the blue Cortina. They're off to dinner.

Now you write your report on what happened during the morning. Begin like this: I took up my position shortly before 8.00 a.m. It was . . .

UNIT 4   Simple Past with AGO

Curriculum Vitae

When someone is applying for a job, they often send a short letter with their *curriculum vitae* attached. Here is the *curriculum vitae* of Howard Morris:

NAME	Howard Morris
SEX	Male
STATUS	Single
DATE OF BIRTH	22/7/48
PLACE OF BIRTH	Dulwich, London

EDUCATION
1953–59	Fairlawn Primary School
1959–65	Sedgehill Comprehensive School

EXAMINATIONS	1962– 'O' Level: English Language, English Literature, History, Geography, French, Mathematics. 1963 – 'A' Level: Mathematics.
1964	Joined *t.t. Texas Warrior*, 50,000 tons, Texas Tanker Company, as officer cadet. Forced to abandon Merchant Navy career owing to failure in eyesight test.
1966	Worked as management trainee, Cadbury Schweppes Ltd.
1967–68	Spent two years on coffee plantation, Kenya.
1969–74	Worked for BBC Bristol.
1974	Transferred to London.

A Oral questions

1 When was Howard Morris born?
2 Where was he born?
3 When did he first attend Sedgehill Comprehensive School?
4 Ask what 'O' Level exams he passed.
5 Answer the question.
6 Ask what he did in 1964.
7 Answer the question.
8 Ask why he left the Merchant Navy.
9 Answer the question.
10 Ask which famous firm he joined in 1966.
11 Ask where he went in 1967.
12 Ask how long he stayed there.
13 Ask when he came back to England.
14 Ask which organisation he joined in 1969.
15 Answer the question.

B   Howard Morris was born in 1948.

(Assume it is now 1978)
He was born thirty years ago.

Say how long ago these things happened to Howard Morris:

1   He first went to Fairlawn Primary School.
2   He first went to Sedgehill Comprehensive School.
3   He took his 'O' Levels.
4   He passed his 'A' Level Mathematics exam.
5   He joined the *t.t. Texas Warrior*.
6   He abandoned his Merchant Navy career.
7   He went to work for Cadbury Schweppes Ltd.
8   He left Kenya.
9   He began to work for the BBC.
10   He transferred to London.

C   Look at this example:

have a drink/ten minutes
I had a drink ten minutes ago.

Use the ideas below to make up more statements with AGO

1   write a letter/two days
2   eat a big meal/three hours
3   travel on a bus/half an hour
4   have a cup of coffee/five minutes
5   go to the cinema/one week
6   listen to the radio/six hours
7   look at a newspaper/five days
8   watch television/twelve hours
9   buy a pair of shoes/ten days
10   see (any person)/one hour

D   This exercise will give you more practice in asking and answering questions in the SIMPLE PAST. Read the story.

A copy of *War and Peace*

John wanted a copy of *War and Peace*, by Tolstoy, so he went to a famous bookshop in Charing Cross Road and asked for it.

The assistant looked puzzled. "I should try the foreign book department," she said.

"But it's a novel, and I want it in English," John replied.

"Oh, novels are on the first floor," she said.

Eventually John found the novels, and after some time he discovered a copy of *War and Peace*.

"I'd like to buy this, please," he said to an assistant in a yellow jumper. She took it from him, and gave him a receipt.

"Pay at the cash desk," she said, pointing vaguely towards the far corner of the shop.

John waited for ten minutes in a small queue, then he paid, and the girl at the cash desk stamped his receipt and gave it back to him.

He took it to the girl in the yellow jumper. She glanced at it and handed him a parcel.

"Thank you," he said.

"Thank you," she replied.

When John got home, he opened his parcel. It contained a book about roses.

1   Ask what John wanted.
2   Answer the question.
3   Ask where he went to buy it.
4   Answer the question.
5   Why do you think the assistant looked puzzled?
6   Where did she advise him to try?
7   Ask what John told the assistant about *War and Peace*.
8   Answer the question.
9   Ask what the assistant in the yellow jumper gave him.
10   Answer the question.
11   What did she tell him to do?
12   Where was the cash desk?
13   Ask what the girl at the cash desk did to his receipt.
14   Answer the question.
15   Ask who he then showed the stamped receipt to.
16   Answer the question.
17   Ask what she gave him.
18   Answer the question.
19   Ask what the parcel contained.
20   Answer the question.

UNIT 4 Simple Past with AGO

E Frankie Sheffield is a famous boxer. Here are some highlights of his career:

1948 Born Leeds, Yorkshire.
1964 Schoolboy Champion of Yorkshire.
1965 Won ABA Junior Championship.
1967 Won ABA Senior lightweight Championship.
1968 Represented England in Olympic Games. Won silver medal.
1969 Turned professional.
1971 Won British lightweight title.
1973 Fought for World title. Beaten on points over fifteen rounds by Dave 'Tiger' Barret of the USA.
1976 Retired as unbeaten British lightweight Champion.

Look at these two conversations:

When did Frankie leave school?
In 1965.
How long ago did Frankie leave school?
(Assume it is 1978) Thirteen years ago.

Do this exercise:

1 Ask when Frankie Sheffield was born.
2. Answer the question.
3 Ask when he became schoolboy champion of Yorkshire.
4 Answer the question.
5 Ask how long ago he won the ABA Junior Championship.
6 Answer the question.
7 Ask when he won the Senior title.
8 Answer the question.
9 Ask how long ago he represented England in the Olympic Games.
10 Answer the question.
11 Ask if he won a medal.
12 Answer the question.
13 Ask when he turned professional.
14 Answer the question.
15 Ask how long ago he won the British title.
16 Ask if he fought for the world title.
17 Ask if he became world champion.
18 Answer the question.
19 Ask what happened in 1976.
20 Answer the question.

F Idea for discussion

Were you an only child? If so, do you regret it? Were you one of a big family? What do you feel about it? Are only children likely to be 'spoilt'? In what way? How much did you learn from your brothers and sisters? What is the difference between being the eldest, the youngest, or one of the in-betweens? How many children would you like to have?

Note how we form the SIMPLE PAST with AGO

STATEMENTS	He It	disappeared	twenty years ago.	
NEGATIVES	He It	didn't (did not)	disappear	long ago.
QUESTIONS	How long ago	did	he it	disappear?

UNIT 4   Simple Past with AGO

Special points to note

The little word *ago* will help you to talk about things that happened in the past, and say *when* they happened. You will only use *ago* with the **past** tense, to talk about a definite and limited point of time.

Examples:

HE CAME BACK FROM UGANDA A WEEK AGO.
THIS LETTER WAS POSTED A MONTH AGO.
HOW LONG AGO DID YOU RECEIVE IT?
SALLY WAS THERE NOT LONG AGO.

WRITTEN SECTION

The Mouse

I live in a big old house. At night you can sometimes hear strange bumps and creaking noises.

Last Saturday I got home late. I crept upstairs, washed and went to bed. My bedroom is very cold and it took me an hour or so to get to sleep.

5   Suddenly I awoke. The room was in darkness, and I could hear a faint scratching sound. It seemed to come from the window. I lay quite still and listened. Then I heard it again: "Scratch, scratch . . . scratch, scratch." It came from the waste paper basket.

I turned on the light beside my bed and the noise stopped at once. I
10   climbed out, shivering, and went over to the waste paper basket. A piece of paper near the top moved ever so slightly. Then I saw a tiny grey face and two little eyes staring up into mine. It was a baby mouse, which had been nibbling away at an old apple core.

What should I do? He just sat there looking at me, as bewildered as I
15   was. Gingerly I picked up the waste paper basket and carried it to the door. Then I opened the door and put it down in the passage outside. I shut the door and went back to bed.

In the morning the mouse had gone.

UNIT 4   Simple Past with AGO

A   **After you have read the story, do the exercise below.**

1   What can you sometimes hear at night in the house where the writer is living?
2   Ask when the writer got home.
3   Answer the questions.
4   Ask how long it took him to get to sleep.
5   Answer the question.
6   When the writer woke up, what could he hear?
7   Ask where the noise came from.
8   Answer the question.
9   What did the writer do that made the noise stop?
10   Why was the writer shivering?
11   Ask what he saw in the basket.
12   Answer the question.
13   What did the writer do with the basket?
14   Was the mouse there in the morning?

B   **Below are some landmarks in English literature. Work out *how long ago* these events occurred.**

1   Shakespeare was born in 1564.
2   He died in 1616.
3   John Keats, the poet, was born in 1795.
4   He died in 1821.
5   Charlotte Brontë was born in 1816.
6   *Jane Eyre* was published in 1847.
7   *David Copperfield* was published in 1850.
8   Dickens died in 1870.
9   *Ulysses* was published in 1922.
10   James Joyce died in 1941.

C   **Read Margaret's story about a visit to Peter Robinson's:**

I'm very annoyed. I saw a blue dress I wanted in the sale in Peter Robinson's. So I got up very early and caught the train to Charing Cross. I took a taxi to Oxford Circus and I arrived there at 7.30. But there was a big queue. At 9 o'clock the store opened and we all rushed in. It was about twenty minutes before I was served, and just as I got to the counter the woman in front of me asked the assistant to take the blue dress out of the window. I hoped they might have some more like it, but they didn't. So I bought a green dress instead. I paid £10 for it and it's horrible. I shall never wear it.

Here are the answers to some questions about the story. You ask the questions.

Example: BY TAXI

         HOW DID SHE TRAVEL TO OXFORD CIRCUS?

1   a blue dress
2   at Peter Robinson's
3   very early
4   by train
5   at 7.30
6   at 9 o'clock
7   to take the blue dress out of the window
8   they didn't
9   a green dress
10   £10

D   **Composition**

Look at the *curriculum vitae* of Howard Morris at the beginning of this unit and write one for yourself.

The Fishing Expedition

I was outside Frank's house at five o'clock sharp, and a few moments later
he came out of the side door, pushing his bike.[1] It didn't take us many
minutes to cycle to the river. We stopped at the bridge, lifted our bikes
over the gate, and hid them behind the hedge.

5   There were some cows in the meadow. They raised their heads, and
looked a little surprised to see visitors so early in the morning. But there
was nobody about, apart from ourselves.

     We reached the island and fixed up our rods. There were a lot of small
fish near the surface, but we didn't catch anything for an hour or so. Then
10   suddenly Frank gave a cry, "Got one!"

     Almost at the same moment something big took my bait,[2] and immedi-
ately made for the reeds under the bank. A moment later the line went
slack. I pulled it up and the hook was gone. But Frank was luckier. "Look
at this," he said happily, pointing to a large Silver Bream, which lay on the
15   bank.

[1] bike: bicycle

[2] bait: a worm or piece of bread

UNIT 5　Some/Any/No　A Little/A Few How Much/How Many

I congratulated him, but felt a bit disappointed about losing my own fish. The sun was up now. It was getting warmer every moment, and there wasn't much point in continuing to fish. I got out the thermos[3] and we drank a little tea and ate a few biscuits.

A　Oral questions

1 Ask what time the writer arrived at Frank's house.
2 Answer the question.
3 Ask how they travelled to the river.
4 Answer the question.
5 Ask where they hid the bikes.
6 Answer the question.
7 What did they do when they reached the island?
8 What did they see near the surface?
9 Why was Frank very happy?
10 Why was the writer a little disappointed?
11 What was in the thermos?
12 What did the men eat?

[3] thermos: flask (which has two glass containers, silvered and separated by a vacuum) for keeping food and drink hot or cold

B　Look at these ideas:

Were there any fish in the river?
Yes, there were some fish in the river.

Were there any crocodiles in the river?
No, there weren't any crocodiles in the river.

Answer the following questions truthfully:

1 Were there any cows in the meadow?
2 Were there any bushes in the meadow?
3 Were there any elephants in the meadow?
4 Were there any trees in the meadow?
5 Was there any grass in the meadow?
6 Were there any wild flowers in the meadow?
7 Were there any sheep in the meadow?
8 Were there any reeds in the river?
9 Were there any other people on the island?
10 Were there any giraffes in the meadow?
11 Were there any sharks in the river?
12 Were there any tigers in the meadow?

C　Look at the exercise above. Pick out the items you answered with negative statements. Express these ideas with *no*

Examples:　THERE WEREN'T ANY CROCODILES IN THE RIVER.

THERE WERE NO CROCODILES IN THE RIVER.

D　Look at this conversation:

How much tea did you buy?
Half a kilo.

How many biscuits did you buy?
I bought a big tin.

Complete the following questions with HOW MUCH or HOW MANY and find suitable replies.

1 . . . coffee did you buy?
2 . . . cakes did he eat?
3 . . . beer did you drink?
4 . . . sugar do you take?
5 . . . bottles of wine did you buy?
6 . . . fruit did you bring?
7 . . . information was he able to give you?
8 . . . money did you spend?
9 . . . petrol did you put in the tank?
10 . . . fish did you catch?

E We say: There was *a little* tea in the thermos.

There were *a few* biscuits in the packet.

Complete the following sentences with There was a little *or* There were a few

1 . . . cows in the meadow.
2 . . . wine in the bottle.
3 . . . people in the theatre.
4 . . . sailors on the ship.
5 . . . snow on the ground.
6 . . . cards on the table.
7 . . . policemen in the square.
8 . . . fog that night.
9 . . . butter in the refrigerator.
10 . . . smoke coming from the chimney.

F We say: Is there *anybody* there?

There isn't *anybody* there.

There is *somebody* there.

Complete the sentences below with <u>anybody</u> *or* <u>somebody</u>:

1 There wasn't . . . in the office.
2 Did . . . answer the phone?
3 . . . took the biscuits.
4 I didn't see . . . there.
5 The manager didn't tell . . . about it.
6 Doris told . . . about it, but we don't know who.
7 There is . . . in the bedroom.
8 Is there . . . in the garden?
9 He said there was . . . in the garage.
10 Did . . . remember the corkscrew⁴?
11 Does . . . like sugar in their coffee?
12 Why didn't . . . tell me about it?

G Idea for discussion

One good reason for going fishing is that it gives us an opportunity to get out into the country, to get close to nature.

There are other things we do, that give us similar opportunities: hunting, camping, walking in the mountains, going for picnics.

Have you ever done any of these things? Talk about them.

Special points to note

We use SOME/SOMEBODY/SOMETHING in affirmative situations:

There is SOME marmalade in the kitchen.
SOMEBODY is coming up in the lift now. . . .
There is SOMETHING I forgot to tell you. . . .

We use ANY/ANYBODY/ANYTHING with negatives.

I can't find ANY milk in the kitchen.
There wasn't ANYBODY in the office.
I'm afraid we haven't got ANYTHING to eat.

and in questions:

Have you got ANY stamps?
Did ANYBODY ask where I was?
Was there ANYTHING interesting in Bob's letter?

We use NO/NOBODY/NOTHING when we wish to make statements that are definitely negative.

I'm sorry, there are NO tickets left for that performance.
NOBODY knew about it.
There was NOTHING more I could do, so I left.

NO statements tend to be stronger than NOT . . . ANY ideas.

We use A FEW with nouns we can count:

There are A FEW grapes in the fruit bowl.
I believe there are A FEW messages for you, Sir.

Similarly, we use HOW MUCH with nouns we can't count:

HOW MUCH sugar did you put in this coffee?
HOW MUCH money did you spend?
HOW MUCH time does it take?

and HOW MANY with nouns we can count:

HOW MANY people watched the game?
HOW MANY biscuits did he eat?
HOW MANY spoonfuls of sugar did you put in this tea?

---

⁴ corkscrew: tool for drawing corks from bottles

UNIT 5　Some/Any/No　A Little/A Few
How Much/How Many

A Trip to Greenwich

We took the boat from Westminster Pier. It was early and there weren't
many other passengers; a few Americans, some Scandinavians and an
Indian family. It was one of those grey, still, autumn mornings, with a
little mist rising from the river.

5 We arrived at Greenwich just after ten o'clock. We wanted to visit the
Cutty Sark[5] at once, but nobody was allowed on board till eleven, so we
decided to walk under the Thames to the Isle of Dogs. There wasn't
anybody else in the tunnel. It was cold down there, and our footsteps
echoed along the damp, tiled walls. From the other side you get a marvel-
10 lous view of the Royal Naval College, built on the site of Henry VIII's old
Tudor Palace.

In the afternoon, the sun came out, and we went up through the park to
the Royal Observatory. By now there were quite a lot of people about.

[5] *Cutty Sark:* a famous sailing vessel of the 19th century,
which was used to transport tea and other goods

15 After visiting the Observatory, and having a cup of tea, we didn't have much time left, but we managed to look round a few of the rooms in the Maritime Museum, before it was time to catch the boat back to London. There was just one disappointment. The Royal Naval College was closed to visitors, so we weren't able to see the famous painted hall. Next time perhaps!

A   Reply to these questions. Use short answers when you can.

1   Where did they get on the boat?
2   Were there many other passengers?
3   Were there any Americans on the boat?
4   What was rising from the river?
5   Why didn't they go on board the *Cutty Sark* as soon as they arrived at Greenwich?
6   How did they get to the other side of the Thames?
7   What was the atmosphere like down in the tunnel?
8   Where did they go in the afternoon?
9   What else did they see that afternoon?
10   What was the disappointment?

B   Complete the following questions with *how much* or *how many*.

1   . . . money did you borrow?
2   . . . tea did you buy?
3   . . . changes did he suggest?
4   . . . change did you bring?
5   . . . books did you buy?
6   . . . sandwiches do you want?
7   . . . beer did he drink?
8   . . . letters did you write?
9   . . . milk did the milkman leave?
10   . . . stamps do you want?

C   Complete the following sentences with:

SOME, ANY, SOMEBODY, SOMETHING, ANYBODY or ANYTHING.

1   Listen! . . . is ringing the bell.
2   Is . . . going to Meg's party tonight?
3   Is there . . . good on the television tonight?
4   Can you lend me . . . money?
5   I promise I won't tell . . . about it.

6   . . . must have his address.
7   Is there . . . milk in the fridge?
8   There is . . . funny about that man.
9   Did . . . see that film last night?
10   I didn't buy . . . in the end.

D   Complete these sentences with *a little* or *a few*.

1   I drank . . . whisky.
2   He smoked . . . cigarettes.
3   I ate . . . biscuits.
4   There was . . . water on the floor.
5   We took . . . photographs.
6   I like . . . tomato sauce with my chips.
7   She made . . . sandwiches.
8   Can I have . . . salt on my eggs?

E   Composition

Write a short composition called *A day in the country*. Describe a real day that you can remember. Begin your composition with "It was . . ."

Journey to Kiel

It was a hot August afternoon, and I had to change trains in Hamburg.

My German was pretty awful. "Kiel?" I asked hopefully, pointing to the train that was about to depart from the next platform. The German porter nodded impatiently and set off with his barrow piled high with
5   suitcases.

Gratefully I climbed in, found myself a corner seat, placed my solitary suitcase on the rack, and sat down. The only other passengers were a short, stout woman with two big shopping bags, and a businessman, wearing a dark blue suit.

10   The train had been travelling for half-an-hour or so, and I was beginning to feel extremely sorry for the businessman, who was perspiring terribly, when the ticket collector came in. He looked at my ticket, waved his arms about a lot, shook his head sadly, gave me back my ticket and departed.

15   The stout woman looked at me sympathetically. "This train Husum", she said. "Not Kiel – Husum." I thanked her.

An hour or so later I got out at Husum, which is practically in Denmark. There I was directed to a small, commuter train, filled with chattering schoolchildren, and in this I travelled across the flat Schleswig-Holstein
20   countryside to Kiel. And believe it or not, in the fields we passed there were real storks, standing lazily on one leg, watching the train go by.

A   Oral questions

1 What was the weather like?
2 Ask where the writer intended to go.
3 Answer the question.
4 Why didn't he go direct from Hamburg to Kiel?
5 Whose fault was it that he got on the wrong train?
6 What did the porter have on his barrow?
7 Describe the two other passengers in the writer's compartment.
8 Why did the writer feel sorry for the business man?
9 Ask if he understood the ticket collector.
10 Answer the question.
11 Who told him the train was going to Husum?
12 What sort of passengers travelled with him on the commuter train?
13 What is the landscape like in Schleswig-Holstein?
14 What did he see from the train?
15 What were they doing?

Adjectives and Adverbs   **Unit 6**

B   Put suitable adjectives in the gaps in the sentences below. (Note: there will generally be more than one correct answer.)

1   "John's been ill, hasn't he?"
    "Yes, he looks _____ ."

2   "Georgina was looking _____ at the party last night, wasn't she?"

3   "I don't think that I'm going to do any work this afternoon, I'm feeling _____ ."

4   "He got very _____ , waiting to be served."

5   "Wasn't that a _____ storm last night?"

6   "The countryside round here is _____ isn't it?"

7   "I lent her my umbrella, but she wasn't at all _____ ."

8   "The dentist was _____ , but he can't do anything till the swelling goes down."

9   "Her husband's that _____ little man over there."

10 "She looked very _____ as she waved him goodbye."

C   Which of the adjectives you have learnt might be useful to describe:

1   A woman?
2   A man?
3   A journey?
4   A car?
5   A small child?
6   A motor accident?
7   A meal?
8   A motor race?
9   A house?
10 A play?

D   Put suitable adverbs in the spaces in the sentences below. (Note: there will probably be more than one correct answer.)

1   It was _____ hot in the train.

2   I slept very _____ last night.

3   "He's gone away," she said _____ .

4   It was _____ midnight, when we got home.

5   She ran _____ to the telephone.

6   "It's _____ late", she said, "I must go home."

7   He climbed _____ up the stairs.

8   The customer banged _____ on the counter.

9   "All right", said the assistant _____ , "I'll serve you in a minute."

10 "Oh, what marvellous news," she cried _____ .

E   Idea for discussion

Practise describing one another. It's interesting to see how far your friend's description of you agrees with your own opinion.

Note how we form adverbs from adjectives

Usually we add **-ly**:

EXAMPLES:

impatient	impatiently
hopeful	hopefully
extreme	extremely

But sometimes it's a little more complicated. If an adjective ends in **-y** we change the **-y** to an **-i** and then add **-ly**

EXAMPLE:

pretty	prettily
lazy	lazily
weary	wearily

A lot of useful adjectives end in **-able**. We change these into **-bly**.

EXAMPLE:

terrible	terribly
impossible	impossibly
probable	probably

Unit 6   Adjectives and Adverbs

A few stay the same.

EXAMPLE

fast	fast

Be specially careful of adjectives which end in **-ly** but are not used as adverbs.

EXAMPLES

lovely	What a *lovely* tune.
lonely	He lives alone in that *lonely* old house.
friendly	The Scots are very *friendly* people.

Special points to note

When we want to describe things or people we use adjectives. Sometimes we put them in front of the noun.

Examples:

HE WAS A <u>BIG</u> MAN.

IT WAS A VERY <u>HOT</u> AFTERNOON.

IT HAD A <u>POWERFUL</u> ENGINE.

WE HAD A <u>DELICIOUS</u> SUPPER.

SHE WAS A <u>STOUT</u> WOMAN.

Sometimes we put them after the noun.

Examples:

THE MAN WAS <u>BIG</u>.

THE AFTERNOON WAS <u>HOT</u>.

THE SUPPER LOOKED <u>DELICIOUS</u>.

THE WOMAN WAS <u>STOUT</u>.

THE COFFEE TASTED <u>AWFUL</u>.

When we want to describe how people do things, we use adverbs.

Examples:

"KIEL?" I ASKED <u>HOPEFULLY</u>.

THE PORTER NODDED <u>IMPATIENTLY</u>.

THE BUSINESS MAN WAS PERSPIRING <u>TERRIBLY</u>.

THE TICKET COLLECTOR SHOOK HIS HEAD <u>SADLY</u>.

THE STORKS STOOD <u>LAZILY</u>, ON ONE LEG, WATCHING THE TRAIN GO BY.

We also use adverbs to modify adjectives and other adverbs.

Examples:

MY GERMAN WAS <u>PRETTY</u> AWFUL.

I WAS BEGINNING TO FEEL <u>EXTREMELY</u> SORRY FOR THE BUSINESS MAN.

IT WAS <u>VERY</u> HOT IN THE CARRIAGE.

WRITTEN SECTION

Tom and Angela

I often think it would be nice to live in the country; to get away from all the smoke and the traffic, and crowds of people in the supermarket, and the long queues at every bus stop; and then I think of Tom and Angela.

5   Tom was a professional soldier, but he got some awful tropical disease while serving in Africa which left him with a permanent limp and a small disability pension[1].

He decided to go in for farming. He went on a year's course and

[1] small disability pension: money paid by the Government to people (especially soldiers) who are ill or injured and who cannot work

managed to rent a small farm, a few miles inland from Folkestone. Occasionally I run down[2] there at the weekend.

10   In the summer it's beautiful. I wander round the fields, inspecting the ripening corn with Tom and his big, brown dog, and lend a hand with the haymaking. In the evening we pop into the cowshed, to watch Angela milking the cows.

But those wretched cows have to be milked every evening. They don't
15   understand about days off, and in the winter, while I, and thousands of lazy people like me, are spending an extra couple of hours in bed, poor old Tom is out feeding them, or trudging wearily from field to field, searching for some miserable beast that has escaped.

I don't think I shall ever become a farmer. There are certain advantages
20   in having a cosy little flat in SW3.[3]

A   Answer these questions:

1   What three disadvantages does the writer mention if you live in town?
2   Why did Tom leave the army?
3   What did the illness leave Tom with?
4   Where is Tom's farm situated?
5   What does the writer sometimes do in the summer time?
6   What is the problem with cows?
7   What do some of them sometimes do?
8   Where does the writer live?

[2] run down: go down occasionally for a short visit

[3] SW3: smart part of London

Unit 6   Adjectives and Adverbs

B   In this unit you have met a number of adjectives and adverbs. Now you will have a chance to check whether you can remember the new ones, and also make sure you have learnt when to use an adjective and when to use an adverb.

Look carefully at this pattern:

GRATEFUL:
a) He smiled _____ at the waitress.
b) He was _____ for the cup of tea.

ANSWERS:
a) gratefully
b) grateful

Now continue in the same way:

1 powerful:
    a) He was a _____ built man.
    b) It was a _____ engine.

2 pretty:
    a) You look very _____ tonight.
    b) The flowers were arranged very
       _____.

3 hot:
    a) The players argued _____ with the referee.
    b) It was a very _____ summer.

4 angry:
    a) George looked _____ at his wife.
    b) George was very _____ .

5 impatient:
    a) Swiss people are sometimes terribly
       _____.
    b) He looked _____ at his watch.

6 awful:
    a) The film was _____.
    b) The film was _____ long.

7 hopeful:
    a) "Shall we go?" Mike looked _____ at Josefina.
    b) The bus driver put down his paper. This was a _____ sign.

8 extreme:
    a) I'm afraid we can expect _____ temperatures over the holiday.
    b) I'm _____ sorry about it.

9 sad:
    a) It was a very _____ occasion.
    b) "No", he smiled, *suddenly* .

10 terrible:
    a) They had a _____ journey.
    b) They're _____ angry about it.

11 lazy:
    a) The boat floated _____ down the stream.
    b) We had a very _____ holiday.

12 nice:
    a) They aren't _____ people, I'm afraid.
    b) He thanked her _____, and went off.

13 sympathetic:
    a) She smiled _____ at her husband.
    b) Dr Barnes has a very _____ manner.

14 miserable:
    a) Stop looking so _____.
    b) She looked _____ at her husband.

15 permanent:
    a) It isn't a _____ job, is it?
    b) He can't stay in there _____.

16 beautiful:
    a) I think it's a _____ song.
    b) It's _____ written.

17 real:
    a) It's _____ gold, you know.
    b) He didn't _____ make it himself.

18 poor:
    a) There are a lot of very _____ people there.
    b) The people were very _____ dressed.

19 weary
    a) He climbed _____ up the hill.
    b) I'm afraid I feel rather _____.

20 cosy:
    a) It's nice and _____ in here.
    b) He turned on the television and they settled down _____ in front of the fire.

C Scrambled descriptions

The police wish to interview two people in connection with a robbery. Unfortunately the descriptions of the two wanted persons somehow got mixed up. See if you can sort them out.

A LORRY DRIVER: Aged about thirty. Slim build, shoulder length fair hair, brown eyes. Dark complexion.
Wearing an oil-stained blue pullover, a tartan mini skirt and black army boots. Carrying a black handbag.

A WAITRESS: Aged about thirty. Broad shouldered, long, dark, curly hair, black moustache, blue eyes. Fair complexion.
Wearing a red jumper, blue jeans and black, high-heeled shoes.

You may need a little help with the vocabulary:

Slim – not fat
Fair – not dark
Complexion – skin colour
Stained – marked
Tartan – Scottish pattern
Broad – wide
Curly – not straight

Now you rewrite the descriptions correctly.

D Composition

Think of a person you admire. Describe what he/she looks like, then write about his/her character and say why you admire him/her.

UNIT 7 *Going to* Future

Bus Conductor Wins Fortune On Pools

This time last week Roy Woods, a bus conductor from Streatham, in South London, was worried about money. He owed £20 to his landlady in rent. Today he is rich, for last Saturday he won £120,000 on the football pools.

5   Last night he was interviewed on television by reporter Stan Edwards.

EDWARDS Well Mr Woods, what are you going to do now? Are you going to give up your job on the buses?

WOODS Yes, I'm going to finish at the end of the week.

EDWARDS And what other plans have you got?

10 WOODS Well, I'm going to buy a house.

EDWARDS Have you got a house of your own now?

WOODS No, no, we live in a furnished flat.

EDWARDS Have you got a car?

WOODS Yes, I've got an old Ford, but I'm going to buy a new

15   car . . . and my wife says she's going to have driving lessons!

A Oral questions

1 What is Roy's job?
2 When is he going to finish working on the buses?
3 Why was Roy worried about money last week?
4 How did he suddenly become rich?
5 Where do Roy and his family live at present?
6 Is he going to buy a new flat?
7 What sort of car has he got?
8 Is he going to buy a new one?
9 What is his wife going to do?
10 Then what do you think she is going to want?

B Oral exercise

Here are the answers to some questions on the text. You ask the questions:

1 Streatham.   Where . . . . ?

2 £20.   How much . . . . landlady?

3 Stan Edwards.   Who . . . . television?

4 Yes, he is.   Is . . . . job?

5 Yes, he is.   Is . . . . a house?

6 No, he doesn't.   . . . . own a house now?

7 Yes, he is.   . . . . a new car.

8 Yes, she is.   . . . . have driving lessons?

C We often use the SIMPLE PAST and the *going to* **FUTURE together like this:**

I went to Canterbury last week, and I'm going to go again tomorrow.

Make similar sentences:

1 I asked for a pay rise last week, and . . . again tomorrow.
2 I had a bath this morning, . . . this evening.
3 I went to the pictures last night, . . . this evening.
4 I saw the doctor yesterday, . . . tomorrow.
5 He won a gold medal at the last Olympics, and I'm sure . . . this time.
6 It rained yesterday, and I think . . . today.
7 You had trouble at Customs last time we went on holiday, . . . again this time.
8 They searched us when we arrived at the airport, and . . . again now.
9 We ran out of milk yesterday, and . . . again today.
10 You grumbled about it yesterday, and . . . again.

D We often use *going to* **in questions like this:**

Where are you going to go for your holiday this year?

Now you make questions:

1 Find out what your friend is going to buy his/her mother for her birthday.
2 It is late at night. You and your friend are at a party. Find out how he/she is going to get home.
3 A girl friend is planning to buy a new party dress. Find out where she is going to buy it.
4 A friend is going to buy a new car. Find out what sort he/she is going to buy.
5 A friend of yours has a boat. He surprises you by saying that he is going to sell it. Find out why.
6 A friend is giving up his job. Find out what he is going to do instead.
7 Your friend announces that he/she is going to get married, but doesn't say who to. Find out the answer.
8 Your friend announces that he/she is going to get married to someone who lives in another town or country. Find out where the couple are going to live.

9 Your friend has a bottle of wine, but no corkscrew. Find out how he/she is going to open the bottle.
10 Your friend has just surprised you by putting a revolver on the table. Find out what he/she is going to do with it.

E Problems

What does George say?
1 You and George arrange to meet Sarah and Emma at 7.30 to go to the pictures. It is 8.00. There is no sign of the girls. George has Sarah's telephone number . . .
2 You and George have been waiting forty-five minutes for a bus. It has just begun to rain. George knows there are taxis waiting round the corner . . .
3 The man next door lit a fire in his garden but he seems to have forgotten it. It is getting bigger and bigger . . .
4 You and George are reading. It is getting dark . . .
5 It is very, very hot. You and George have been playing tennis. George knows there is some beer in the refrigerator . . .
6 George likes Dundee cake very much. He knows there is some in the cake tin . . .
7 George has just had a tax rebate. The carpet in the sitting-room is getting very old. He is looking at it . . .
8 A few days ago George met Christine . He thinks she is a wonderful girl. She isn't married and neither is he . . .
9 The electricity workers went on strike last year and there were awful power cuts. George knows that the electricity workers are still not happy about their pay. Winter is approaching . . .
10 George can't drive. But he's decided that life would be much nicer if he had a licence and a car.

F Sometimes we use *I'm not going to* **to express an argument very forcibly. Look at this example:**

You are at a political meeting with a friend. You disagree strongly with what the speaker is saying. You say:
  "I'm not going to listen to any more of this rubbish!"

UNIT 7 *Going to* Future

Study the situations below and make similar remarks:

1 You think the programme on the television is awful.
   I'm not _____ rubbish.

2 The last time your friend borrowed your camera he broke it.
   You're not _____ again.

3 Last time you let your friend pick the apples from your tree, he dropped half of them and bruised them.
   You're not _____ *my* tree!

4 Yesterday evening your friend refused to let you watch a TV programme at his house. Now *he* wants to watch a programme in yours.
   You're not _____ *my* television.

5 Last time you lent your watch to your friend, he dropped it.
   I'm not _____ .

6 You and your friend are going out with the same boy/girl. Your friend wants to ring that person up.
   You're not _____ *my* phone!

7 Your friend arrives at your house with a record you *hate* in his hand.
   You're not _____ *my* record player.

8 You are passing a fruit shop and your friend suggests you should buy some fruit. But the last time you bought fruit at that shop it turned out to be very poor quality.
   I'm not _____ *that* shop.

Idea for discussion

Ask the person next to you what he or she is going to do:

this afternoon; this evening; tomorrow; on Saturday; next Sunday.

Answer the questions. Then talk about some more things you are going to do in the next few days.

Note how we form the *going to* future:

STATEMENTS	I'm She's etc.	going to	buy	a new car.

NEGATIVES *Note:* We sometimes say: *He isn't going to buy . . .* *You aren't going to buy . . .* etc.	I'm She's etc.	not	going to	buy	a new car.

QUESTIONS	Am	I		
	Are	you	going to	buy a new car?
	Is	he/she		
	Are	we you they		

38

Special points to note

The *going to* future is probably the most useful future tense in English. We use it every time we want to talk about something we intend to do.

Examples:

I'M GOING TO GIVE UP MY JOB.

HE'S GOING TO BUY A HOUSE IN LONDON.

IS LUCY GOING TO BUY THAT COAT?

I'M NOT GOING TO GO TO THE PARTY.

Notice that we treat *going to* almost as if it was one word, and we DON'T stress the word *going*.

The *going to* future is also used when predicting that things are going to happen:

I think it's going to rain this afternoon.
I'm sure John isn't going to pass the exam.

WRITTEN SECTION

Susanne's Job

TONY   What are you going to do when you go home? Have you got a job waiting for you?

SUSANNE   No, I gave up my job when I came here. I worked in a shipping office, but I decided I needed a change.

5   TONY   What are you going to do then? Are you going to try and get a similar job with another firm?

SUSANNE   No, I'm going to try and get a job with a travel firm. That's why I need English. In the other job it was documents, documents, all day long. Now I'd like a job where I'm dealing

10   with people.

A   Answer these questions

1   Has Susanne got a job waiting for her?
2   What sort of office did Susanne work in?
3   Ask why she gave up that job.
4   Answer the question.
5   Is she going to get a similar job with another firm?
6   What sort of a firm would she like to work for?
7   Does she want a job where she will be dealing with people?
8   What didn't she like dealing with in the other job?

UNIT 7   *Going to* Future

B   Look at this sentence:

She gave up her job when she came to England, but she's GOING TO get another one.

Now make similar sentences, using going to:

1   He sold his car, but . . . .

2   He divorced his last wife, but . . . .

3   They lost their cat, but . . . .

4   I smoked your last cigarette, but . . . .

5   We went to Scotland for our holiday last year, but . . . .

6   I'm afraid I broke one of your cups, but . . . .

7   I missed the train yesterday, but . . . .

8   I saw the film about a year ago, but . . . .

C   Note this pattern:

Tony wonders if Susanne intends to get a new job. He says:

Are you going to get a new job?

Now you ask the questions:

1   Susanne isn't well. You wonder if she intends to see a doctor.

2   There is a bottle of wine on the sideboard. It has been opened but Susanne seems to have forgotten it.

3   Susanne borrowed an umbrella from a friend. She lost it. You wonder if Susanne intends to replace it.

4   Susanne had a very nice friend called Mary. Mary has just gone to Canada. You wonder if they are going to keep in touch.

5   You are at the seaside with Susanne. You wonder if she intends to come for a swim.

6   It is late, but there is an exciting horror movie just beginning on television. You want to know if Susanne intends to watch.

7   You want a bath, but you know Susanne wants one too. You wonder if she intends to have one now.

8   You are hungry. You wonder if Susanne intends to cook something.

D   Composition

This is what the fortune teller told your friend Mary:

"You are generally happy, but you're a bit restless. You're never going to be rich, but you're not going to be terribly poor either. You're going to travel. You're going to go somewhere very hot. You're going to have an illness and you're going to spend some weeks in hospital. Be careful about the water you drink. Very soon you're going to meet somebody who's going to be very important in your life."

Now imagine you are the fortune teller. Use the notes below to tell your friend's fortune.

Change job; money; journey; new friends; accident; a lucky year; marry; children; achieve a secret ambition; live to a very old age.

Henry

"Henry!"

"Yes, dear?"

"I'm going up to bed now. Don't forget to do your little jobs."

"No, dear."

5   Henry turned off the television and went into the kitchen. He fed the cat, washed up several dishes, dried them and put them away. Then he put the cat out, locked all the doors and turned out all the lights. When he got

to the bedroom, his wife was sitting up in bed reading a book and eating chocolates.

10　"Well dear, have you done all your little jobs?"

"I think so, my love."

"Have you fed the cat?"

"Yes, dear."

"Have you put him out?"

15　"Yes, dear."

"Have you washed up the dishes?"

"Yes, dear."

"Have you put them all away?"

"Yes, dear."

20　"Have you tidied the kitchen?"

"Yes, dear."

"Have you turned out all the lights?"

"Yes, dear."

"Have you locked the front door?"

25　"Yes, dear."

"Then you can come to bed."

"Thank you, dear."

After a little while they heard a gate banging downstairs.

"Henry."

30　"Yes, dear."

"I'm afraid you've forgotten to shut the garden gate."

"Oh dear! . . ."

A　Questions on the text

1　Where did Henry's wife say she was going?

2　What was it that Henry did for the cat that probably pleased it?

3　What was it that Henry did to the cat that probably didn't please it?

4　What did Henry do to the doors?

5　What did he do to the lights?

6　What was Henry's wife doing when Henry reached the bedroom?

7　What was the noise that Henry heard after he had got into bed?

8　What did he have to do about it?

B Look at this pattern:

Done . . . .
I've done all my little jobs.

Imagine you are Henry. Make up similar sentences, using the ideas below.

1 Fed . . . .
2 Put . . . . out.
3 Washed up . . . .
4 Put . . . . away.
5 Tidied . . . .
6 Turned out . . . .
7 Locked . . . .
8 Forgotten to . . . .

C Henry's wife might say:

He hasn't done all his little jobs yet.

Make up similar sentences, using the ideas in B.

D At the end of Henry's conversation with his wife, she says:

I'M AFRAID YOU'VE FORGOTTEN TO SHUT THE GARDEN GATE.

I'M AFRAID . . . often means I'M SORRY, BUT . . .

Use the notes below to make similar sentences:

1 I/break/glass
2 We/drink/all the wine
3 I/lose/my key
4 I/forget/to bring any money
5 They/eat/all the cake
6 You/miss/train
7 I/throw/it away
8 I/quarrel/with Andy
9 They/finish/the biscuits
10 I/forget/your name

E Read the story of Jack Arnold's life. Then do the exercise below:

Jack Arnold is sixty-six now. He has led a very exciting life. This is what he told me:

I've sailed round the world twice, I've worked on a tea plantation, I've hunted big game in Africa, I've driven a racing car at Indianapolis, and I've appeared in four films.

I've taken part in two revolutions, I've ridden in the Grand National, I've spent six months in a Chinese jail, and I've had four wives. But I've never killed anyone, and I've never been to Russia.

1 What sort of life has Jack had?
2 Ask if he's sailed round the world.
3 Answer the question.
4 What does he say about a tea plantation?
5 What does he say about big game?
6 Ask if he's ever been to Indianapolis.
7 What does he say about films?
8 Ask if he's taken part in any revolutions.
9 What famous race has he ridden in?
10 Ask if he's ever been to jail.
11 Answer the question.
12 Where?
13 How many men has he killed?
14 **How long did he spend in Russia?**
15 How do you know that he likes being married?

F Idea for discussion

Look again at some of the details of Jack Arnold's life. Yours probably hasn't been as exciting as his so far, but there's plenty of time yet! Think of some things you have done, places you've been, etc. and talk about them.

UNIT 8   Present Perfect

Note how we form the PRESENT PERFECT:

STATEMENTS	I've		turned out	the lights.
	He's			
	etc.			

NEGATIVES	I	haven't	turned out	the lights.
	He	hasn't		
	etc.			

QUESTIONS	Have	you	turned out	the lights?
	Has	he		
	Have	they		

Note: the reply to this question is *Yes, I have*, or *No, I haven't* not *Yes, I've.*

Special points to note

When you have mastered the **present perfect,** you will be able to talk about:

a) things that have or haven't *just* happened
b) things which have or haven't happened, when you are *not* interested in the time factor.

Examples:

HAVE YOU TURNED OUT THE LIGHTS?

YES, I HAVE, or NO, I HAVEN'T.

HAVE YOU EVER BEEN TO JAPAN?

I'VE NEVER EATEN THIS SORT OF FISH BEFORE.

OH, DEAR. I'VE (JUST) DROPPED THE KEY.

Problem:

Many students confuse the **simple past** with the **present perfect**. (Unit 14 will help with this problem.)

Meanwhile remember:

Native English speakers *never* use the **present perfect** with a point of time in the past.

We sometimes say things like:

"Have you seen him this week?"
"Yes, I've talked to him this morning."

But in these cases we are regarding "this week" and "this morning" as uncompleted periods of time.

Read the story of David Irvin

David Irvin is an actor. He's never been a star, but he's appeared in more
than fifty films during the last twenty years.

    Usually he's played the part of a minor villain, and very often he has
become an unfortunate victim of fate. In fact he has 'died' in more than
5 thirty films.

    David said: "They've shot me thirteen times, they've drowned me
twice, they've run me over with a car on seven occasions, and I've fallen to

my death from six high buildings. Apart from that I've been burnt to
death, I've died three horrible deaths from drinking poison, and finally
10 I've had my head chopped off. Still I must say I've enjoyed it all tremend-
ously."

A   Do this exercise:

1   What is David's job?
2   Ask if he's ever been a star.
3   Answer the question.
4   Ask how many films he's appeared in during the last twenty years.
5   Answer the question.
6   What sort of parts has he played?
7   Ask how many times he's 'died'.
8   Answer the question.
9   Ask how many times he's been shot.
10 Answer the question.
11 Ask if he's been run over by a car.
12 Answer the question.
13 Ask if he's ever fallen from high buildings.
14 Ask if he's ever drunk poison.
15 Ask if he's enjoyed his time in the film industry.

Present Perfect

B Look at this idea:

South America/Africa
I've been to South America, and now I'm going to go to Africa.

Use the ideas below to make up similar sentences:

1 wash shirt/iron
2 teach India/Saudi Arabia
3 take photograph your sister/you
4 tidy kitchen/sitting room
5 visit Rome/Florence
6 sell furniture/house
7 read book/see film
8 see show/buy record
9 type letters/tidy desk
10 buy stamps/post letters

C Situations. Look carefully at this example. Then do the exercise:

THE TRAIN LEAVES AT 8.45. MR AND MRS SMITH ARRIVE AT THE STATION AT 8.50. WHAT DOES MR SMITH SAY?

"WE'VE JUST MISSED THE TRAIN".

1 John took an examination a few days ago. He has just looked at the list of successful students. He has a happy smile on his face. Why?
2 The football fans are jumping up and down with joy. What have their team just done?
3 Mr Jones got home from work one summer evening and said to Mrs Jones: "I think I'll cut the grass." In fact the man next door asked Mrs Jones if he could borrow the lawn mower half an hour before. He is using it now. What does Mrs Jones say?

4 Sid and his wife are going to Spain for their holiday. Sid comes home with some air tickets in his hand. What does he say?
5 David's car needs a service. He hasn't used it to come to work today. What does he say?
6 When June comes home from school, she usually lets herself in with her own key. Today she can't find it. What does she say when her mother opens the door?
7 David and Christine are standing in the foyer of the theatre looking very miserable. All the seats are sold. The performance is going to begin in four minutes, and David can't find the tickets. What's happened?
8 Howard was due to play football this afternoon, but his ankle is swollen and bandaged. He's telephoning the captain of the team. "I can't play today", he says. What reason does he give?
9 Last week Keith smoked a lot of cigarettes. People keep offering him cigarettes and he keeps saying "No, thank you." "Why?" they ask. What is his answer?
10 Frank is asking Louise to go with him to see *The Return of Frankenstein*. Louise saw it on television last year, so she refuses. What does she say?

D Composition

Think of an uncle, real or imaginary, and write about some of the things he's done, places he's been to, things he's never done and places he's never been to.

UNIT 9 Present Perfect with Since and For
Present Perfect Continuous

Fred

Fred is a guardsman. He's been standing on guard outside the gates of Windsor Castle for the last two hours. He has just been relieved. The sergeant of the guard has noticed that Fred is looking rather miserable.

	SERGEANT	What's the matter with you, lad? Stop looking so glum.
5	FRED	I've been having a terrible time, sergeant. Those tourists have been getting me down.
	SERGEANT	Don't you like being a tourist attraction then?
	FRED	Well, you expect it in the summer, but at this time of the year . . . I've had all the witty ones today . . . Is he
10		real? . . . Why isn't he in Madame Tussaud's? . . . I saw his eyes move . . .
	SERGEANT	Cheer up lad! Have a cup of tea and think of all that beautiful foreign currency you've been earning.

A Oral questions

1 Ask where Fred has been standing.
2 Answer the question.
3 Ask who's noticed that he's looking miserable.
4 Answer the question.
5 Ask if Fred has been enjoying himself.
6 Answer the question.
7 Ask what's been getting him down.
8 Answer the question.
9 Ask what sort of tourists have been looking at Fred today.
10 Answer the question.
11 Ask what they've been doing that's upset him.
12 Answer the question.
13 Ask what the sergeant's told him to do.
14 Answer the question.

B When the sergeant asked Fred why he was looking so glum, Fred replied:

I'VE BEEN HAVING A TERRIBLE TIME, SERGEANT. THOSE TOURISTS HAVE BEEN GETTING ME DOWN.

Look at another example of the same sort of idea:

GEOFF ARRIVES AT THE OFFICE, RED IN THE FACE, AND DRIPPING WITH PERSPIRATION. HE MIGHT SAY:

I'VE BEEN RUNNING or I'VE BEEN RUSHING or I'VE BEEN HURRYING.

Look at some more situations and make similar remarks about them:

1 James comes into the kitchen with muddy knees and feet. He has a football under his arm.
2 Sally's mother comes into the sitting-room. Sally is looking at her doll's house. All the furniture is arranged very nicely.
3 Christine is coming out of the bedroom. The beds look very neat and tidy.
4 Frank is covered in oil. The car is outside and he has been outside too.
5 Pat is coming in from the garden. She has a basket full of apples. The apple tree is at the end of the garden.
6 Howard is interested in birds. He is coming in from the garden. He has a pair of binoculars.
7 Josefina likes cooking. She is coming out of the sitting-room. On the table near the sofa is a copy of *Home Cooking*.
8 Valerie is near the record player. She is putting a record of *Carmen* back into its sleeve.
9 Louise is wearing her blue bikini. She is walking away from the sea. She and her bikini are wet.
10 Sid is near the television. It was on. Now it is off.
11 David has an ashtray near him. He is the only person in the room who smokes, and there is ash in the ashtray.
12 Jack is near the telephone. The receiver was in his hand. Now it is back on its hook.

C In the story about Fred, notice the sentence:

He's been standing on guard outside the gates of Windsor Castle FOR TWO HOURS.

Here is another situation where we need to use the same construction:

Mrs Green put a cake in the oven at 11.0 o'clock. It's now 11.30.
   The cake has been baking FOR HALF-AN-HOUR.

Make up similar sentences:

1 Rod is waiting to take a photograph. He was in position at 9.30. It is now 9.45 and he's still standing there.
2 Jack is fishing. He began at 6.00 am. It is now 11.00 am.
3 Richard is working on his motor bike. He started at 11.00 o'clock. Now it is 1.00 o'clock.
4 Mike is in the launderette. He arrived at 4.00 pm. But all the machines were being used. It is now 4.30, and none of the machines are free yet.
5 Kathy began to type Mr Allen's report at 10.00 am. It is now 12.30 and she is still working on it.
6 The newspaper seller first sold newspapers outside Paddington station in 1956. He's still selling them in the same spot.
7 Mike bought his first record when he was sixteen. He's forty-six now and he's still buying records.
8 John collects stamps. His first stamps were given to him when he was seven. He's thirty-seven now.
9 Keith Smith is a boxer. He had his first fight when he was fifteen. He's twenty-five now and he still boxes.
10 Mr Dean took out a driving licence when he was nineteen. He's sixty-nine now and he's still driving.
11 Mr Horn first taught when he was twenty. Now he's sixty, and he's still teaching.
12 Lanfranc rebuilt Canterbury Cathedral shortly after 1066. The Cathedral is still standing on the same spot.

UNIT 9   Present Perfect with Since and For Present Perfect Continuous

D   Look at these ideas:

KATIE BECAME A BARRISTER IN 1973. SHE WORKS AS A BARRISTER NOW. SHE'S BEEN A BARRISTER <u>SINCE</u> 1973.

JOHN BEGAN TO WRITE A BOOK IN 1975. HE'S STILL WORKING AT IT. HE'S BEEN WORKING ON HIS BOOK <u>SINCE</u> 1975.

Now use the notes below to express similar ideas:

1   Richard got a job as a clerk with the Electricity Board in 1972. He still works there.
2   Joe became a professional jockey in 1960. He's still riding.
3   Pete bought his first car in 1956. He still drives a car.
4   Frank moved to Sheffield in 1950. He still lives there.
5   The old oak tree was planted in 1745. It is still standing on the village green.
6   They played a crude form of football in England in the Middle Ages. The game is still popular.
7   Tom began to collect stamps when he was twelve. He still collects stamps.
8   Colonel Allen started painting watercolours when he was a young officer. He still paints watercolours.
9   Keith had his first French lessons when he was twelve. He's seventeen now and he's still learning French.
10   Sylvia had her first guitar lesson when she was nine years old. She still plays the guitar.

E   Look at this conversation:

JOHN   How long have you been living in London?
ALICE   For two years.
JOHN   Where do you work?
ALICE   In the city.
JOHN   Is it an interesting job?
ALICE   Oh, not too bad – I'm a secretary in a solicitor's office.
JOHN   How long have you worked there?
ALICE   Since last February.

1   Where does Alice live?
2   How long has she lived there?
3   What sort of an office does she work in?
4   How long has she worked there?

Now find two possible answers to the following questions, one with <u>since</u> and one with <u>for</u>:

1   How long have you lived at your present address?
2   Think of a friend who is married. How long has he/she been married?
3   Think of a friend who works. How long has this friend worked in his/her present job?
4   Look at your shoes. How long have you had them?
5   Think of a friend who has a car. How long has he/she had it?
6   Think of a family pet. Say what the pet is, and how long the family have had it.
7   Name your home town and say how long you have lived there.
8   Think of a friend and say how long you have known him/her.
9   Think of a famous sportsman/sportswoman. Say how long he/she has been famous.
10   Say whether you have a bank account or savings account. How long have you had it?

F   Idea for discussion

Some crimes are obviously more serious than others, and sometimes the punishment does not seem to 'fit the crime'.

In England some of those who took part in the famous Great Train Robbery were sentenced to thirty years in prison. They stole money. Yet murderers sometimes get sentenced to life imprisonment and they get out of prison much sooner than this.

Once we had capital punishment in England. We don't any more. Some people think it should be brought back. Do you think these people are right?

What is the real purpose of sending people to prison?

Tell us about experiments with 'open' prisons and the treatment of prisoners in your country.

Present Perfect with Since and For
Present Perfect Continuous

Note how we form the **PRESENT PERFECT** with *since/for*:

STATEMENTS	I've He's	been here	since 1970. for ten years.

NEGATIVES	I haven't He hasn't	been here	since last Christmas. for six months.

QUESTIONS	Have you Has she	been here	since two o'clock? for an hour?

Note how we form the **PRESENT PERFECT CONTINUOUS:**

STATEMENTS	I've She's	been waiting	since 9.30. for a long time.

NEGATIVES	I haven't She hasn't	been waiting	since 9.00 o'clock. for a long time.

QUESTIONS	Have you Has he	been waiting	since 9.00 o'clock? for a long time?

NOTE ALSO:	How long	has she	been waiting?

UNIT 9   Present Perfect with Since and For
Present Perfect Continuous

Special points to note

By using the **present perfect** + **since/for** construction you will be able to state accurately, or find out how long something has or hasn't lasted.

Examples:

HOW LONG HAVE YOU LIVED IN LONDON?
(WE'VE LIVED HERE) FOR TEN YEARS.

HOW LONG HAS HE WORKED FOR THIS FIRM?
(HE'S WORKED FOR THIS FIRM) SINCE 1970.

Remember:

since + a *point* in time   (1970)
for + a *length* of time   (ten years)

We use the **present perfect continuous** to talk about a period of time with a present connection and present results.

Examples:

Are you still learning English?
Oh yes, I've been learning English for six months now.

How long have you been working?
I've been working for three hours and I'm tired out now.

Note: in these examples, the activities began in the past – but we are interested in what is happening now.

Note also how we can use the **present perfect continuous** to make negative statements:

I haven't been working on this job since last July.

But statements like this can be ambiguous. This could mean:

a) that the speaker is working on the job for the first time since last July
b) that the speaker wants to make it clear that he has done other things apart from working on this job since last July.

You will also find that **present perfect continuous** is often used to explain how a situation came about.

Why are you looking so hot?
I've been running.

Present Perfect with Since and For Present Perfect Continuous

On the banks of the Amazon

A television team working on a programme about the Amazon have just discovered a young Oxford undergraduate living with a primitive tribe of Indians. They interviewed him for their programme.

	INTERVIEWER	Of course we were very surprised to discover a white man living here. What exactly are you doing?
5		
	YOUNG MAN	I've been living in this village for about six months. I'm studying the lives and customs of these people, and I'm going to write a book about it.
	INTERVIEWER	And have you learnt a lot?
10	YOUNG MAN	Oh, yes. I've been sharing the daily lives of the inhabitants. I've been on their hunting expeditions. I've taken part in their rituals and festivals. I've learnt to understand their language. I feel they have really begun to trust me.
15	INTERVIEWER	And how long do you plan to stay?
	YOUNG MAN	Well, that depends on various factors. I've been here since last September. I plan to stay until next August at least, but possibly a bit longer.

A Do this exercise

1 Ask what the camera team have found.
2 Answer the question.
3 Ask who the young man has been living with.
4 Answer the question.
5 Ask how long he has been living there.
6 Answer the question.
7 Ask what he's been doing.
8 Answer the question.
9 Ask if he's learnt much.
10 Answer the question.
11 Ask what he's been sharing with the inhabitants.
12 Answer the question.
13 Ask if he's been on any hunting expeditions.
14 Answer the question.
15 Ask if he's learnt to speak their language.
16 Answer the question.
17 Ask if he thinks the people have come to trust him.
18 Answer the question.
19 Ask if he's decided exactly when he's going to return to civilisation.
20 Answer the question.

UNIT 9 Present Perfect with Since and For Present Perfect Continuous

B Note these ideas:

I've lived here FOR two years
I've been living here FOR two years
I've worked there SINCE February
I've been working there SINCE February

Put SINCE *or* FOR in the following sentences:

1 He's been living there . . . July.
2 She's been waiting . . . an hour.
3 He's had a driving licence . . . 1971.
4 I haven't been to the theatre . . . last Christmas.
5 John has worked here . . . two years.
6 I haven't heard from her . . . a fortnight.
7 He's been in hospital . . . last May.
8 She hasn't written . . . nearly three months.
9 That church has been standing there . . . the Normans came to Britain.
10 Our team haven't won a match . . . the beginning of the season.

C Complete the following sentences:

1 I haven't played tennis for . . . .
2 She's worked in this office since . . . .
3 He's had that watch since . . . .
4 I haven't been to France for . . . .
5 We haven't met for . . . .
6 It's been there since . . . .
7 It hasn't been there for . . . .
8 He's been dead for . . . .
9 I haven't felt well since . . . .
10 It's been snowing for . . . .

D Composition

Imagine that you are sitting in a restaurant at a station in your own country, and you get into conversation with an African sociologist, who is in your country studying the subject of *marriage customs*. (How young people usually meet, where they live after they get married, how old they are when they marry, how many children they have, if there is divorce, etc.)

Write the conversation you might have with him. Begin like this:

You   Where do you come from?
A.S.   From Nigeria.

The Commonwealth

Once Britain had an Empire, but that Empire ceased to exist long ago, and now the Commonwealth has taken its place. This is a voluntary club of independent countries, which continued to have a special relationship with one another after they gained their independence from Britain.

5   People of many different colours and religions belong to the Commonwealth. Ten per cent are of European descent, ten per cent are African, while Asians make up the largest group, totalling some six hundred million people.

The Commonwealth is one of the most democratic organisations in
10   existence. Each country has complete freedom to express its own opinion about world affairs, and when the heads meet, they never take a vote. They discuss matters and come to an informal agreement. This seems a much more sensible system than that employed in some other international organisations.

15   However, the Commonwealth contains so many different sorts of people, from so many different parts of the world, that inevitably there are disagreements. But it does not seem unreasonable to say, as Prince Philip once said, that ". . . the Commonwealth is the nearest thing we have to the Brotherhood of Man".

A Oral questions

1 Ask what Britain once had.
2 Answer the question.
3 What has taken its place?
4 Which people make up the largest group?
5 How much freedom does each country have to express its own opinion about world affairs?
6 What did Prince Philip once say about the Commonwealth?

UNIT 10 Comparatives and Superlatives

B Look at this idea:

This seems a *more sensible* system *than* that employed in some other organisations

It's a *better* system *than* the one we use . . .

Use the ideas below to make up more comparative sentences:

1 Peter has made two records. The first sold 5,000 copies. His new one has sold 10,000 already.
(POPULAR)

2 When our football team played last week, the score was 0–0, and the crowd were very silent. This week they played again. The score was 3–3, and the crowd shouted all the time.
(EXCITING)

3 You can get a big pot of marmalade at the supermarket for 50p. It costs at least 60p at the corner shop.
(EXPENSIVE)

4 Yesterday the temperature was just above freezing. Today it is one degree below freezing.
(COLD)

5 The children were happy yesterday, but not as happy as they are today.
(HAPPY)

6 I had to pay 35p for tomatoes last week. This week I had to pay 40p.
(DEAR)

7 The music next door was loud last night, but not as loud as it is this morning.
(LOUD)

8 This is a nice house, but not as nice as the one we lived in before.
(NICE)

9 Angela is small for her age, but not as small as Kitty.
(SMALL)

10 Agnes is pretty, but not as pretty as Barbara.
(PRETTY)

11 Mr Fox is short, but not as short as his brother.
(SHORT)

12 The *Frankenstein* film was frightening, but not as frightening as the *Dracula* film.
(FRIGHTENING)

C Look at these ideas:

There are a number of democratic organisations I know of. But none are more democratic than the Commonwealth.

The Commonwealth is *the most democratic* organisation I know of.

Yesterday the temperature was −2°C. It hasn't been so cold this year.

Yesterday was *the coldest* day of the year.

The world has seen many remarkable men, but none more remarkable than Schweitzer. I interviewed him once.

He's *the most remarkable* man I've ever interviewed.

Use the ideas below to make up more superlatives:

1 Mrs Smith has three sons. They are all clever, but Peter is outstanding.
(CLEVER)

2 I've seen many exciting films, but never one more exciting than *The Birds*.
(EXCITING)

3 There are fourteen cars in the race. The Ferrari did 160 kph in practice. No other car reached that speed.
(FAST)

4 I've read many interesting books, but I found Maugham's autobiography specially interesting.
(INTERESTING)

5 There were several old players in the cricket team, but Mr Green was fifty-nine. All the other players were in their thirties or forties.
(OLD)

6 Italy has produced many fine tenors, but none with a more magnificent voice than Caruso. I heard him once.
(MAGNIFICENT)

7 There are several mountains in Wales, but none of them are as high as Snowdon.
(HIGH)

8 I've seen many marvellous footballers, but Pelé was exceptional.
(MARVELLOUS)

9 Several of the nurses in the hospital were kind, but Nurse Goode was specially kind.
(KIND)

10 There have been many successful English writers, but none more successful than Charles Dickens.
(SUCCESSFUL)

D   Note this idea carefully:

Peter earns £14 a week. John earns £12 a week. John earns LESS THAN Peter.

Use the ideas below to make up similar sentences with LESS THAN

1 The oranges cost 7p each. The lemons cost 6p each.

2 A football match lasts ninety minutes. They had played for eighty-five minutes, and the score was 0–0 when Beckenbauer scored.

3 These black shoes cost £8. These brown ones cost £12.

4 Tom started last week with £4 in his pocket. He still had £1 and a few pence at the end of the week.

5 George lost a lot of weight when he was ill. When he stood on the scales, the needle didn't reach the fifty-one kilogram mark.

6 The Smiths have a very nice house. But they bought it a long time ago and the price they paid was under £3,000.

7 Peter has a new Ford Fiesta. It uses very little petrol. He put four gallons in the tank and went to Oxford. There were still more than two gallons in the tank when he got there.

8 George went to see the doctor. He expected to be with him for half-an-hour, but he came out after twenty-minutes.

9 Angela and Kitty went to Sue's birthday party. There were a lot of nice things to eat. Angela ate a lot, but Kitty didn't eat so much.

10 The population of London is bigger than that of Switzerland.

E   Look at these ideas:

. . . the Commonwealth contains SO MANY different sorts of people . . . THAT . . . there are disagreements.

There was SO MUCH fog THAT it was impossible for planes to take off or land.

Note: We use MANY with countable nouns, and MUCH with uncountable nouns.

Use the ideas below to make up more sentences containing so much *or* so many.

1 There are a lot of pigeons in Trafalgar Square. It's impossible to feed them all.

2 A lot of people wanted to see the tennis. It was difficult to get a ticket.

3 There were a great many customers in the store. It was impossible to serve them all quickly.

4 There was a lot of traffic. The bus took half-an-hour to get from Charing Cross to Piccadilly Circus.

5 There were a lot of people at the football match. It was almost impossible to see unless you were very tall.

6 There were a lot of tourists in the city. It was very difficult to find a hotel room.

7 It rained a lot. The streets became flooded.

8 There are a lot of films on in the West End. It's difficult to choose one.

9 There were a great many people at the airport. It was almost impossible to find anyone.

10 There were a lot of people in the queue. It was impossible to get on the bus.

F   Read this text:

Peter can run the One Hundred Metres in 10.1 seconds. However his friend Paul can do it in ten seconds. So Peter can't run the One Hundred Metres AS FAST AS Paul.

Now express the ideas below using   *as . . . as*

1 Yesterday the temperature was 13°C. Today it is 15°C.

2 Mr Parker often arrives late at the office. Yesterday he arrived at 9.35. It is 9.15 and he is just coming in through the door.

UNIT 10   Comparatives and Superlatives

3   Mrs Smith cooks excellent meals for her students. The dinner today is very good, but yesterday it was even better.

4   The examination the students are doing is hard. But the last one was even harder.

5   The firemen have been called to a big fire in the city. Last week they were called to another one. That was even bigger.

6   King George V came to the throne in 1910. He died in 1936. His son, George VI, became King in 1936 and reigned till 1952.

7   Tom Curtis is a poet. He published a book recently, but only 740 copies have been sold. His friend Lionel Crawford also published a book of poems. Only 400 copies have been sold.

8   Peter is a young policeman. He only took home £70 last week. Next door to him lives a milkman called Harry. Harry took home about £90 last week.

9   Frances can speak French, German and some Spanish, but her sister Judy speaks all three fluently, and she can make herself understood in Russian and Italian.

10 George has been to Germany, Italy and France, but Tom has been to the USA, Mexico and Venezuela as well.

Ideas for discussion

When we are talking about different sports we often use comparisons and superlatives. Look at these examples:

Football is more exciting than cricket.
Ski-ing is more dangerous than football.
It was the most exciting game I've ever seen.

Make a list of sports and games that interest you and compare them in this way.

Special points to note

When you want to compare two things or people, you will need the **comparative**.

Examples:

A MORE SENSIBLE SYSTEM THAN . . . .

A MORE BEAUTIFUL LANDSCAPE THAN . . . .

AN OLDER SYSTEM THAN . . . .

A PRETTIER PICTURE THAN . . . .

When you want to compare three or more things or people, you will need the **superlative**.

Examples:

THE MOST DEMOCRATIC ORGANISATION

THE MOST MARVELLOUS PERFORMANCE

THE COLDEST DAY

THE HAPPIEST GIRL

When you want to compare things in a negative way, you will use *less*.

Examples:

A LESS BEAUTIFUL CAR THAN . . . .
A LESS SYMPATHETIC DOCTOR THAN . . . .

When you want to compare how things are done, you will again need the **comparative**.

Examples:

SHE RAN FASTER THAN SHE DID LAST TIME.

IT WILL RUN MORE SMOOTHLY IF YOU PUT A BIT OF OIL ON IT.

For **negative comparisons**, again you will use *less*.

Examples:

HE LOOKED AT ME LESS ANGRILY . . . .

SHE PAINTS LESS FREQUENTLY NOW.

Note the useful phrases SO MUCH THAT and SO MANY THAT.

Examples:

THERE WERE SO MANY LOCUSTS THAT IT WAS IMPOSSIBLE TO KILL THEM ALL.

THE TEA COST SO MUCH THAT EVEN THE ENGLISH WERE DRINKING COFFEE.

Note also the AS . . . AS construction

Examples:

SHE WENT AS WHITE AS A SHEET WHEN SHE HEARD THE NEWS.

HE RAN AS QUICKLY AS POSSIBLE TO THE NEAREST TELEPHONE BOX.

Finally learn these very unusual comparisons carefully:

good well	better	best

This is a GOOD cup of coffee, but the one we had this morning was even BETTER.

David ran WELL, Geoff ran even BETTER, but Tom ran BEST of all.

bad ill badly	worse	worst

It was a BAD accident this morning, but the one last night was even WORSE.

The boys have measles. Richard is quite ill, Anthony is WORSE, and Dicky is the WORST of the three.

I backed three horses. Night Nurse ran BADLY, The Dikler ran WORSE, and Fort Devon ran the WORST of the three.

A Visit to the Gallery

If you visit palaces or stately homes in England, and look at the pictures painted in the 16th and 17th centuries, you will find that all the most famous painters had foreign names, which is not surprising, for they were nearly all foreigners.

5   It may be for this reason that foreign visitors are surprised to find that Britain has produced so many interesting painters since that time.

William Hogarth was the first great English artist to have his work reproduced in quantity. Prints of all his most important work can be seen in the little house where he lived at Chiswick.

10   Turner and Constable were born a few years after Hogarth died. They are both painters deserving a world-wide reputation, two of the greatest landscape painters in the history of art. Contemporaries, yet so different in temperament: Constable, shy and quiet, painting to please himself, and Turner, the business man, with his extraordinary energy, a far more

15   extrovert personality.

Then there are the great portrait painters, Sir John Lavery the Irishman, and Reynolds the friend of the rich and famous, and that most astonishing of all religious painters, William Blake.

There are so many that it is impossible to mention them all, but during

20   the last two hundred and fifty years Britain has produced a rich assortment of artistic talent.

1   Why did all the painters who painted in England in the 16th and 17th century have foreign names?

2   Where can prints of most of Hogarth's work be seen?

3   When were Constable and Turner born?

4   Who was the extrovert?

5   What can you say about Constable?

6   What did Reynolds paint mostly?

7   Was Lavery English?

8   What sort of a painter was Blake?

B Look at these ideas:

Turner was a MORE EXTROVERT personality than Constable.

Constable was a MUCH QUIETER man than Turner.

Look at the ideas below and write one **comparative** *sentence like this for each.*

1 Kevin plays the guitar, but not as well as George.
2 It's hot. We're both thirsty, but I'm not as thirsty as you.
3 I watched *Play of the Week* on television last night. It wasn't as interesting as the play last week.
4 Pelé is popular in Europe, but he is a hero in South America.
5 Andy is intellectual, but not as intellectual as Dan.
6 The lecture is very boring. Tom is bored, but not as bored as Mike.
7 Tony is quite polite. His brother Jack isn't polite at all.
8 The old Datsun was quite fast, but not as fast as the new model.
9 The last band was loud, but not as loud as the one playing now.
10 Tom's sister is thin, but not as thin as Tom.

C Look at these ideas:

All the MOST FAMOUS painters had foreign names.
. . . two of the GREATEST landscape painters in the history of art.

Use the ideas below to make up sentences containing **superlatives:**

1 Last night there was a terrible storm. Nobody could remember a worse one.
2 Rita is a very ungrateful girl. In fact I can't remember meeting anyone as ungrateful as her before.
3 Last night we saw a marvellous new production of *Carmen*. I can't remember seeing such a marvellous production before.
4 Frank took Maria to the dance. There were a lot of pretty girls there, but Frank didn't think any of them were prettier than Maria.
5 Cyril is very lazy. I've never met anyone as lazy as him.
6 I met a scientist called Tubby Rice last night. I haven't met anyone who interested me more for a long time.
7 Tom told me of the break-up of his romance with Liz. I haven't heard such a sad story for ages.
8 I went to a party last Saturday. I haven't been to such a noisy party for a long time.
9 When I first came to work in the office, I felt rather strange and lonely. Several people were kind and helpful, but none more so than Patricia.
10 We went out and had a delicious meal last night. I haven't had such a delicious meal for a long time.

D Composition

Write a short composition comparing the lives of two men doing very different jobs: a farm labourer and a bank clerk perhaps, or a shop assistant and a teacher.

Write about the hours they work, the money they earn, their working conditions.

Perhaps you could interview two men doing different jobs and so write about real people.

UNIT 11   Simple Future

Paul and Terry

Paul was having a drink with some of his colleagues from the office, when suddenly he looked at his watch.

PAUL   Blast! Is that the time?

TERRY   **It's just ten to seven – why?**

5 PAUL   **I've got an appointment – I'm meeting a friend in London at eight o'clock. I'll never make it.**

TERRY   I'm going into London. I'll give you a lift if you like.

PAUL   Could you really? That would be kind.

TERRY   Where are you meeting your friend?

10 PAUL   Near Piccadilly – but if you can drop me at an underground station, that'll be fine.

TERRY   No, it's all right, Piccadilly's not far out of my way, I'll take you there.

PAUL   That's very kind of you.

A   Questions on the text

1 Who was Paul having a drink with?
2 Ask what he looked at.
3 Answer the question.
4 What time was Paul's appointment?
5 What did Terry offer to do?
6 Where did Paul plan to meet his friend?
7 Where does he say Terry can drop him off?
8 What does Terry say he'll do?

B Note this idea:

I'M GOING *into* London. I'LL GIVE you a lift.

Use this form to offer help to your friend in the following circumstances:

1 You are seeing Mr Smith this evening. Your friend would like a message given to him.
2 You are going to the record shop. Your friend hears a certain record on the radio and says, "I must get a copy of that record."
3 You have an appointment with the dentist this morning. Your friend has a problem with his teeth.
4 You have to go to a big store this afternoon. Your friend would like to know if they have any cheap tennis racquets.
5 You intend to write to Alice this evening. Your friend would like you to send her his best wishes.
6 You have to visit the baker's shop. You know that your friend needs a loaf of bread.
7 You plan to ring Joan this evening. Your friend hopes that she and her sister will come to the party on Saturday evening.
8 You are going out. You know you will pass a letter box. Your friend has just written a letter and put the stamps on it.
9 You are going to the Plaza cinema this evening. Your friend would like to know which film is showing next week.
10 You have to go to London. You intend to go by train. Your friend has to go to Coventry the next day. He would like to know what time the train leaves.

C There are occasions when we are forced into a defensive position. In these situations *Don't worry, I'll* . . . can be a useful defence. Study this conversation.

SHE   You haven't cleaned the car.
HE   I know, I'm sorry, I've been busy.
SHE   We're going to Jenny's party tomorrow.
HE   I know.
SHE   I hate arriving at their house with the car all dirty. You know what Jenny's like . . .
HE   All right. Don't worry, I'll clean it tomorrow morning!

Now defend yourself in the same way from the following accusations. Begin: Don't worry, I'll . . .

1 You promised to take those photos in to be developed!
2 You haven't rung your brother yet!
3 You didn't write that letter yesterday!
4 You forgot to get any milk!
5 You haven't found out when that film is on!
6 You didn't get those tickets today, did you?
7 You haven't got your suit back from the cleaner's yet!
8 You didn't get a film for the camera, did you?
9 You didn't take your shoes to be repaired!
10 You didn't get any batteries for the radio, did you?

D *Giving the bad news.* Here are some situations where your friend is hoping something is possible. You know it isn't. Give him the bad news, using *won't*

Example:

You are sitting in a train with your friend. You hoped to get home early as you had been invited to a party. But the train has been held up and you don't expect to get home till nearly midnight.

WE WON'T GET HOME IN TIME FOR THE PARTY.

1 Your friend wants tickets for a pop concert. You know the tickets were sold out ages ago.
2 Your friend hopes he might get a train direct from Oxford to Cheltenham. You are sure he will have to change trains.
3 Your friend thinks Sushee might go out with him. You know she is engaged to a very nice Indian boy.
4 Your friend wants a pair of rather expensive brown leather shoes. He thinks he might get them at the local shoe shop. You know they only stock cheap shoes.
5 You are at a football match with your friend. Your team are losing 1–0. There are only two minutes to go, and your team don't look like scoring.
6 Denis is only twenty-two. He has applied for a position of great responsibility. You and your friend are sure he is too inexperienced to get the job.

UNIT 11 Simple Future

E **We often express a similar idea by using:**
You'll never . . .

You and your friend know another student who is not very intelligent and doesn't work hard either.

You might say: HE'LL NEVER PASS THE EXAM!

Go back to Exercise D and use these ideas to produce remarks beginning: YOU'LL NEVER . . . , HE'LL NEVER . . . etc.

F **People often make indirect requests. Sometimes we ignore them, but at other times we offer to do what the other person wishes, using:** *Shall I . . . ?* like this,

BOSS   My goodness, it's hot in here.
SECRETARY   Shall I open the window?

Reply to the following remarks. Begin with: SHALL I . . . ?

1   We've run out of aspirins.

2   A cup of coffee would be nice.
3   Oh, dear, I don't feel at all well.
4   I wish I knew Mr Fox's telephone number.
5   I wonder what the fare to Edinburgh is.
6   This typewriter doesn't seem to be working properly.
7   Oh, look, melons. I love melons.
8   I want a nice photograph of myself, to send my mother.
9   Gracious, it's cold in here.
10   My goodness, it's pouring with rain. How *am* I going to get to the station?

G   Idea for discussion
Imagine that you are going to have a class party one evening next week. Everybody must volunteer to do something, bring something, or organise something so that the party will be a success. Explain what you will do to help. (Use the *I'll* form.)

Note how we form the SIMPLE FUTURE:

STATEMENTS	I'll He'll etc.	ring	for an ambulance.

NEGATIVES	I	shan't won't	tell	George about it.
	You	won't		
	He/she	won't		
	We	shan't won't		
	You/they	won't		

QUESTIONS	Shall	I	tell	George about it?
	Will	you		
	Will	he/she		
	Shall	we		
	Will	you		
	Will	they		

Special points to note

We have already met the *going to* future in unit 7, and the *present continuous* as a future in unit 2.

The *going to* future is used when we want to say that we intend to do something:

I'M GOING TO BUY SOME NEW SHOES TOMORROW.

The present continuous used as a future is a very definite statement, usually about an arrangement which has been made:

WE'RE GOING TO THE THEATRE THIS EVENING. (You already have the tickets).

You will need the **simple future** when there is a problem, and you can offer a solution. Paul had an appointment. He was afraid he was going to be late, but Terry said:

I'LL GIVE YOU A LIFT.

Incidentally, the **simple future** is usually the last tense you use when saying *goodbye* to a friend:

BYE, I'LL SEE YOU TOMORROW

CHEERIO, I'LL RING YOU IN THE MORNING.

WRITTEN SECTION

An Accident On The Motorway

It was winter and there was ice on the roads. Mr Jones was driving down the motorway, when he saw a car, upside-down, at the side of the road. He pulled onto the hard shoulder and stopped. Another car drew in¹ behind him and stopped too.

5   Mr Jones and the other driver hurried to the spot where the car lay.
    "The driver's still inside. He's unconscious," said Mr Jones. "I'll go and telephone for an ambulance."

¹ drew in: drove to the side of the road and stopped

UNIT 11 Simple Future

"I'm afraid his legs are trapped. You'd better phone for the police and the fire brigade as well," suggested the other man.

10 "Righto." Mr Jones ran back to his car, jumped in, and drove off. He found a telephone box half a mile down the road and dialled 999.

"Emergency, which service do you require?" asked the operator.

"All three," replied Mr Jones.

A Answer these questions

1 What did Mr Jones see at the side of the motorway?
2 What did the car behind do?
3 What did Mr Jones and the other driver do after they got out of their cars?
4 In what condition was the driver of the crashed car?
5 What did Mr Jones say?
6 What was the problem regarding the driver's legs?
7 What suggestion did the driver of the second car make to Mr Jones?
8 Where did Mr Jones find a telephone box?
9 Who answered the telephone?
10 What question did the operator ask Mr Jones?

B Note this sentence:

I'll go and telephone for an ambulance.

Imagine you are Mr Jones. Reply to the following suggestions or questions concerning the driver of the crashed car, using the I'll form.

1 The driver says he is thirsty.
2 The driver would like you to send a message to his wife.
3 The driver is worried about some important papers in his briefcase.
4 The driver would like you to come and visit him in the hospital.
5 The driver wonders if you could stay with the car till the breakdown truck arrives.
6 The driver ask you to look after an antique silver cigarette box he just bought. It is in the boot.

C Note this pattern:

Your friend is finding it difficult to open a bottle.
You say: I'LL OPEN IT FOR YOU.

Offer to do more things for a friend, using I'LL.

1 Your friend looks cold.
2 Your friend is reading, and the room is getting dark.
3 You think your friend might be thirsty.
4 Your friend has written a letter. He can't find an envelope.
5 You think your friend might be hungry.
6 Your friend has to catch a train. You have a car.
7 Your friend is short of money.
8 Your friend took a jacket to be cleaned. You are going near the cleaner's.
9 Your friend has two heavy suitcases.
10 Your friend is about to go home. He has no umbrella, and it's pouring with rain.

D   Composition

You work for an international firm, with its head office in New York. One of the American directors, James D. Kapp, writes to your boss, saying that he is coming to your country for a short visit. Mr Kapp plans to stay for fourteen days, from 1st to 14th May. His trip is to be part business/part vacation. He intends to spend the first week in your capital city, and the second week travelling about the country.

He wants a hotel room booked for his wife and himself, he wants arrangements made for the hire of a self-drive car, and he wants a route suggested, that he might follow, to take in some of the most interesting sights in your country. Your boss puts Mr Kapp's letter on your desk, with a brief note: "Deal with this please."

Write to Mr Kapp, promising to do as he requests, and suggest a route he might follow, and places he might visit. Begin your letter "Dear Mr Kapp" and end it "Yours sincerely", with your own signature. Use your own address (or the address of your school), writing it on the right hand side of the top of the page. Write today's date below the address, like this:

> 9 London Street,
> Harrow,
> Middlesex,
> England
> 22 May 1979

Dear Mr Kapp,

_____

_____

_____

_____

_____

_____

_____

_____

_____

_____

Yours sincerely,

(Your signature)

UNIT 12 Auxiliaries (Modals) I

CAN/COULD/MAY/MIGHT/I'D RATHER/WANT TO

Tom and Stella

Tom and Stella want to get married, but they can't find anywhere to live.
Unfortunately Tom doesn't earn a large salary.

TOM   Don't worry dear, we'll find something soon.

STELLA   Perhaps we could get a mortgage and buy a house.

5 TOM   Houses are terribly expensive.

STELLA   Do you think your mother might let us make a flat upstairs in her house?

TOM   I don't really want to ask her, I'd rather find a place of our own.

STELLA   Well, get the local paper again tomorrow. There may be some

10   flats to let advertised there.

TOM   All right, I can telephone from the office.

STELLA   Yes, but if there is anything that might be suitable, ring first thing in the morning,[1] you know how quickly they go.

A Oral questions

1 What do Tom and Stella want to do?
2 What are they looking for?
3 Ask if Tom earns a large salary.
4 What does Stella suggest they might do?
5 What is Tom's reply?
6 How does Stella think that Tom's mother might help?
7 What is Tom's reply?
8 What does Stella tell Tom to do?
9 Ask if Tom agrees.
10 Answer the question.
11 Where does Tom say he can telephone from?
12 What does Stella tell him to do?

68   [1] first thing in the morning: as early as possible

CAN/COULD/MAY/MIGHT/I'D RATHER/WANT TO

B Look at these two ideas

I CAN telephone from the office.
Perhaps we COULD get a mortgage.

Note that it would be possible to reverse CAN and COULD; however, the meaning would change slightly, because COULD is a more tentative suggestion than CAN.

I COULD telephone from the office.
Perhaps we CAN get a mortgage.

Now make more suggestions using can *or* could *in the following situations.*

1 It is raining. You and your friend have a free afternoon. There is a good film on.
2 You and your friend are a bit tired. Sometimes you stay at home in the evening.
3 You need some money urgently. You have a car worth £500.
4 You and your friend are waiting in a hotel lounge. An hour ago you had a pot of coffee. You think a fresh pot of coffee would be a good idea.
5 You need some money in a hurry. Sometimes it is possible to borrow money from the bank.
6 You and your friend run a small business. You had a burglary six months ago and another last night. Burglars are afraid of guard dogs.
7 You and your friend would like to find au pair jobs. Sometimes you can get a job like this through an agency.
8 Another way of finding a job like this is to put an advertisement in the paper.

Try and think of some more situations where WE CAN . . . or WE COULD . . . might be useful.

C Look at these ideas

There MAY be some flats to let advertised there. Do you think your mother MIGHT let us make a flat upstairs?

MAY and MIGHT are both used to express the idea PERHAPS, or IT IS POSSIBLE.

Use the ideas below to make *two* sentences.

a) With MAY suggesting a 50 per cent possibility
b) With MIGHT suggesting a 30 per cent possibility

1 It's possible that you will get a letter from Emily this week.
2 A new TV would be expensive. Perhaps they will be able to repair the old one.
3 There are black clouds in the sky, but it's possible that it won't rain.
4 You want a copy of a certain book. You find you can't get it locally. Perhaps you will get a copy in the city.
5 Your friend has 'flu[2] and doesn't feel at all well. But this sort of 'flu doesn't last long.
6 You are wondering what you will do next year. You are not very happy with your present job. There are often good opportunities abroad.
7 You hurt your back playing tennis. You have seen two doctors, but your back is still painful. An osteopath can sometimes help in situations like this.
8 You want a copy of the *Radio Times*. They don't have one at the local shops, but sometimes the bookstall at the station has a lot of copies.

Now think of some things you may or might do in the next few weeks.

D Look at these ideas

Tom and Stella WANT TO get married.
I'D RATHER find a place of our own.

WANT TO and I'D RATHER are often used in the same conversation like this:

PETER   I want to see the film at the Odeon.
MARY   Do you? I'd rather see the one at the Plaza.

Now use the ideas below to make similar conversations:

1 watch television/listen to the radio
2 go by air/go by ship
3 have a cup of tea/ . . . coffee
4 talk about the exam/ . . . our holiday
5 get a job in London/ . . . Paris
6 go to the football/ . . . greyhound racing
7 see *The Beast with Two Heads*/ . . . *Terrors of the Night*
8 go to the seaside/ . . . go into the country

Can you think of any more conversations like this?

E   Look at this conversation:

COULD YOU POSSIBLY POST THIS LETTER FOR ME?
OF COURSE. or I'M AFRAID NOT, I'M NOT GOING
    PAST A LETTER BOX.

Use the ideas below to make similar conversations:

1   Your friend wants you to stay in this evening.
2   Your friend wants you to buy her some stamps.
3   Your friend wants you to give a message to George.
4   Your friend wants you to buy some chocolate biscuits.
5   Your friend wants you to take the dog for a walk.
6   Your friend wants you to fetch her skirt from the dry-cleaner's.
7   Your friend wants you to lend him £5 till Monday.
8   Your friend wants you to take a film to be developed.
9   Your friend wants you to get a bottle of milk.
10 Your friend wants you to turn the radio down.

F   Look at this conversation:

I don't really want to go out.
Oh, would you rather stay at home?

Use the notes below to make similar conversations:

1   play tennis/go to the cinema
2   go to the theatre/watch television
3   play cards/listen to some records
4   watch television/listen to the radio
5   go to the cinema/stay at home
6   watch this programme/see the film on the other channel
7   meet David and his girl friend/go for a walk
8   do any more work now/go for a drive

G   Idea for discussion

Finding a home can often be a problem for a young married couple. Imagine you have enough money to buy a bit of land, and design and build your own bungalow. (A little house, on one floor only.) Draw your plan and talk about it as you do so.

Note how we form sentences, using these auxiliaries:

STATEMENTS	I	can	telephone	him tomorrow.
		could		
	she	may		
		might		
	etc.	'd rather		
		want to		

NEGATIVES	I	can	not	telephone	him tomorrow.
		could			
	she	may			
		might			
	etc.	'd rather			

Note: We often use CAN'T and COULDN'T

I/we	don't want to	telephone him.

Auxiliaries (Modals) I

UNIT 12

CAN/COULD/MAY/MIGHT/I'D RATHER/WANT TO

QUESTIONS

Can	I	telephone tomorrow?
Could		
May	he	
Might	etc.	

But:
Do you want to telephone him?

Special points to note

Can/Could

Technically COULD is the past of CAN.

Example:

I CAN SEE THE COAST OF FRANCE.
HE SAID HE COULD SEE THE COAST OF FRANCE.

In this example CAN means IT IS POSSIBLE, and COULD means IT WAS POSSIBLE.

However CAN is often used instead of MAY when asking for permission, like this:

CAN I GO TO THE DANCE?
NO, YOU CAN'T, YOU'RE TOO YOUNG.

We also use CAN and COULD to make suggestions:

PERHAPS WE COULD GO BY AIR.

May/Might

Similarly MIGHT is the past of MAY:

MAY I GO TO GEORGINA'S PARTY?
I SAID YOU MIGHT.

But look at this use of MAY and MIGHT:

HE MAY TELEPHONE ME THIS EVENING.
HE MIGHT TELEPHONE ME THIS EVENING.

Here both MAY and MIGHT convey the PERHAPS idea. Note that MAY is a little more probable than MIGHT.

Want To

I WANT TO means I WISH TO.

Very often, in order to be polite, we use I'D LIKE TO instead.

However there are occasions when you will want to express a wish in a direct way. Then WANT TO is useful.

Examples:

I WANT TO GO HOME NOW.
I DON'T WANT TO HEAR ANY MORE ABOUT IT.

I'd rather

I'D RATHER means I'D PREFER TO.

"WOULD YOU LIKE A WHISKY?"
"I'D RATHER HAVE A CUP OF TEA."

"I'D RATHER NOT GO OUT THIS EVENING."

UNIT 12 Auxiliaries (Modals) I

CAN/COULD/MAY/MIGHT/I'D RATHER/WANT TO

Richard and Joan

	RICHARD	Where shall we go for our holiday this year?
	JOAN	We're going to Spain, aren't we?
	RICHARD	No, let's have a change. I'm tired of Spain.
	JOAN	We can go to Greece if you like.
5	RICHARD	No, I want to get away from the Mediterranean, I'd rather have a holiday in the country.
	JOAN	Well, what about Switzerland? We could rent a chalet up in the mountains.
10	RICHARD	I'm afraid that might be pretty expensive, and anyway I'd rather go somewhere we haven't been before.
	JOAN	Tibet?
	RICHARD	Don't be silly, I'm serious . . . I was thinking of Finland.
	JOAN	Isn't it rather cold and dark there?
15	RICHARD	Not in the summer. They have dozens of fantastic lakes and marvellous pine forests . . . if you're lucky you may run into a big brown bear.
	JOAN	A wild one?
	RICHARD	Yes, I believe there are still a few.
	JOAN	All right, see if you can get some brochures. . . .

A Do this exercise

1 Where does Joan think they are going for their holiday?
2 Why doesn't Richard want to go to Spain or Greece?
3 What sort of holiday would he rather have?
4 What are his objections to renting a chalet in the Swiss mountains?
5 Why does he accuse Joan of being silly?
6 What impression does Joan have of Finland?
7 What two features of the Finnish landscape does Richard mention?
8 What animal does he say Joan might run into?
9 Ask what Joan tells him to get.
10 Answer the question.

Auxiliaries (Modals) I

CAN/COULD/MAY/MIGHT/I'D RATHER/WANT TO

Sent, Switzerland

B Read the conversation below and then fill each gap with one of the auxiliaries listed. Use each auxiliary once only.

can/'d rather/might/could/can't

DAVID   I'm not going out now, it (1) rain.

ANNE   Don't be so silly, you (2) take an umbrella.

DAVID   I don't like umbrellas, I always lose them.

ANNE   Well, I (3) you didn't lose this one – it was expensive.

DAVID   It's pink – I (4) go out with a pink umbrella.

ANNE   Look, I must have that meat, or there won't be any lunch.

DAVID   We (5) have frozen fish, or something like that.

ANNE   I haven't got any.

C Look at this conversation:

DO YOU WANT a coffee?
I'D RATHER have an orange juice.

Reply to the following suggestions using I'd rather . . .

1 Let's go to an Indian restaurant.
2 Shall we play tennis this afternoon?
3 Let's paint the door red.
4 Would you like to watch television?
5 Do you want a coffee?
6 Come for a walk.

D Composition

Imagine that your firm is sending you to London for a year to work. You want to rent a flat. Write to an estate agent in London explaining what you want. (How many rooms, what part of London etc.) Begin your letter: "Dear Sir" and end it: "Yours faithfully".

UNIT 13 Auxiliaries (Modals) II

MUST/MUSTN'T/NEEDN'T/OUGHT TO/HAD BETTER

MUST/MUSTN'T/NEEDN'T/OUGHT TO/HAD BETTER

Liza

Liza is Mrs Ross's au pair. One Sunday evening she came back from London looking very upset.

	MRS ROSS	What's the matter dear?
5	LIZA	Something awful happened. We went to the Portobello Road and someone stole my handbag.
	MRS ROSS	Oh, dear, did you lose a lot of money?
	LIZA	No, only a few pounds, but my passport was in the bag. That's what I'm really worried about.
10	MRS ROSS	You must tell your embassy about it and I think they'll issue you with a new one.
	LIZA	I'd better go tomorrow.
	MRS ROSS	No, you needn't go tomorrow, but you mustn't leave it too long. Did you report it to the police?
	LIZA	No, I couldn't find a policeman.
15	MRS ROSS	Well, you must report that it's been stolen and give the police a description of your handbag. You'd better go to the local police station tomorrow morning.
	LIZA	Perhaps I could go to the embassy on Saturday?
20	MRS ROSS	They might not be open on a Saturday, so you ought to ring them to check first.
	LIZA	Yes, I'll do it tomorrow.
	MRS ROSS	And Liza . . .
	LIZA	Yes?
	MRS ROSS	Don't be too upset . . . it's not the end of the world.

A Oral questions

1 What is Liza's job?
2 What happened to her in the Portobello Road?
3 Ask if she lost a lot of money.
4 Answer the question.
5 What else did she lose?
6 Where can she get a new one?
7 Where must she go on Monday?
8 Why?
9 When might she go to the embassy?
10 What ought she to do first?

UNIT 13 Auxiliaries (Modals) II

MUST/MUSTN'T/NEEDN'T/OUGHT TO/HAD BETTER

B Look at these ideas:

You must tell your embassy
You ought to ring them . . .
You'd better go to the local police station tomorrow morning.

Note that all three of these are interchangeable, but by changing them we alter the meaning of the sentence.

YOU MUST TELL YOUR EMBASSY ABOUT IT is an urgent recommendation in this text, though it is usually an order.

YOU OUGHT TO INFORM YOUR EMBASSY is a strong recommendation

YOU'D BETTER INFORM YOUR EMBASSY is a piece of advice

You are speaking to a friend. Make up three sentences for each situation below.

1   see/dentist/tomorrow
2   speak/doctor/about it
3   complain/manager
4   take it back/shop
5   write/to him tomorrow
6   ask/day off
7   tell Jack/deal with it
8   send her/telegram
9   telephone/hotel
10 have/a few days off

C Look at this pattern:

A professional footballer
train very hard/smoke

A professional footballer MUST train very hard.
A professional footballer MUSTN'T smoke.

Say what these people must or mustn't do.

1   The driver of a car
    have a licence/drive without a licence
2   A doctor
    study for a long time/practise without being qualified
3   A teacher of English for foreigners
    speak too fast/speak clearly
4   A hospital nurse
    be kind and understanding/too upset at the sight of blood

5   A passenger on British Rail
    have a ticket/travel without a ticket
6   A visitor to the zoo
    pay at the entrance/feed the monkeys
7   A bus driver
    drive too fast/drive very carefully
8   A shop assistant
    be rude to the customers/be familiar with the goods she's selling
9   A referee
    know the rules of the game/be afraid of making unpopular decisions
10 A policeman
    accept bribes[1]/be honest

D Look at this pattern:

tomorrow/you can go on Saturday
You needn't go tomorrow, you can go on Saturday

What other things needn't your friend do?

1   any coffee/we have plenty
2   your key/I've got mine
3   lock . . . door/we'll be back in a few moments
4   wait . . . landlady/you can leave her a note
5   umbrella/it isn't going to rain
6   money now/you can pay me later
7   coffee for me/I've just had my tea
8   any money/the shops will all be closed
9   reserve seats/it's not a very popular play
10 get . . . stamps/I found some

E Give your friend some advice in the following situations.
Use *you'd better* . . .

1   I only bought these shoes last week and this heel has come off already.
2   This tooth hurts when I drink anything cold.
3   I sent the money off for those theatre tickets two weeks ago. I still haven't heard anything, and the performance is on Friday.

[1] bribes: presents which are given to somebody so that he will do something he shouldn't do

4   The milkman forgot to deliver any milk today.
5   Oh, dear. I forgot to take that book back to the library.
6   It's some time since this suit was cleaned.
7   Bother, I didn't post that letter to the bank.
8   Oh, I forgot to send my sister a birthday card and it's her birthday tomorrow.

F   Idea for discussion

In big cities there are thieves, and they often steal from foreign visitors. What advice would you give your young brother or sister, who was going abroad for the first time?

Are there special places where a visitor must be careful? Is it more dangerous at night? How much cash should one carry? What is the advantage of having traveller's cheques?

Note how we form sentences, using these auxiliaries:

STATEMENTS

I	must	write to him.
she	need(s) to	
etc.	ought to	
	'd better	

NEGATIVES

I	mustn't	write to him.
she	needn't	
etc.	oughtn't to	
	'd better not	

QUESTIONS

Must	I	write to him?
Need	he	

But: Ought   I (etc) *to* write to him
       Had   I (etc)   better   write to him?

Points to note

Must

MUST is usually an order, but it can be an urgent recommendation.

YOU MUST DO IT TOMORROW!

Note that MUSTN'T is always an order:

You MUSTN'T tell him about it.

To express the idea IT ISN'T NECESSARY, we use NEEDN'T.

YOU NEEDN'T DO IT TODAY.
YOU NEEDN'T WRITE TO HIM, I'LL DO IT.

Ought to

OUGHT TO is a strong recommendation.

YOU REALLY OUGHT TO SEE A DOCTOR ABOUT YOUR LEG.
YOU OUGHT NOT TO WORK SO HARD.

I'd better

I'D BETTER means IT WOULD BE A GOOD IDEA TO.
I'D BETTER PHONE HER THIS EVENING.

When said to someone else, it is a useful way of giving advice:

YOU'D BETTER TELL ME ALL ABOUT IT.
YOU'D BETTER NOT TELL GEORGE.
YOU'D BETTER TURN OFF THE GAS.

77

UNIT 13 Auxiliaries (Modals) II

MUST/MUSTN'T/NEEDN'T/OUGHT TO/HAD BETTER

WRITTEN SECTION

Khady Seck

Khady Seck[2] was going into the centre of London for the first time. "Now," she said to herself, "I mustn't forget to insure my camera."

Khady came from Senegal. She had spent a month in Paris before coming to London, and while she was there she had bought herself a fairly expensive 8 mm movie camera. A friend told her that she must get it insured. She knew that this was good advice, so she went into a camera shop near Piccadilly Circus.

ASSISTANT Afternoon . . . can I help you?

KHADY Yes, I bought a Bolex movie camera in Paris recently and I think I ought to insure it.

ASSISTANT Yes . . . er . . . we can arrange for it to be insured . . . um . . . which model is it exactly?

KHADY A super 8, with a battery.

ASSISTANT Yes, but I'll need the model number and the serial number.

KHADY I'm not sure where the serial number is . . . I think I'd better bring the camera in . . .

ASSISTANT No, you needn't bring the camera in . . . you'll find the serial number on the guarantee form.

KHADY Have you any idea how much it'll cost?

ASSSISTANT It depends which model it is.

KHADY All right. Thank you . . . I'll see you next week.

A Do this exercise

1 Ask where Khady came from.
2 Answer the question.
3 What was it that Khady didn't want to forget?
4 Ask where she bought the camera.
5 Answer the question.
6 Who advised her to insure it?
7 Where did she go to ask about it?
8 What information did the man in the shop need?
9 Where did the assistant suggest Khady should look for the serial number?
10 What other information did Khady ask for?

[2] Khady: pronounced Haddy

B Put *mustn't* or *needn't* in the gaps in the following sentences:

1 You _____ give Freddy any more sweets or he won't eat any tea.

2 The Doctor said I _____ go back to the hospital; my leg is all right.

3 You _____ make any sandwiches for me. I'm not hungry.

4 She _____ fill in a new application form, we have the other one.

5 You _____ mention this to Kate, or she'll get upset.

6 She _____ bring a doctor's certificate, she was only away for one day.

7 You _____ take any more aspirins, you've had four already.

8 Tell her she _____ open any letters marked "personal".

C Here are five situations where you will be able to use the auxiliaries you have been practising. Use each auxiliary only once.

must/mustn't/ought to/needn't/'d better

1 There's a fantastic film on at the Odeon. Advise your friend to see it before it's too late.
2 Tell your friend not to drive her car till it's insured.
3 You are going to play tennis with a friend at the tennis club. Tell him it isn't necessary for him to bring any tennis balls as the club supply them.
4 Your friend has just received his bank statement. He's sure it's incorrect. Advise him to telephone the bank.
5 Tell your Venezuelan friend that she needs a visa to get into France.

D **Composition**

WATCH YOUR PURSE

Write a short notice to be handed to foreign visitors to your country warning them to look after their money and valuables.

UNIT 14   Simple Past v Present Perfect

Doris and Belinda

Doris and Belinda are traffic wardens. It's their job to keep the traffic moving and see that people don't park where parking is forbidden.

"I'm going to book this one," said Doris.

"He hasn't been there long, has he?" objected Belinda.

5 "He's been there too long," replied Doris. "Anyway he shouldn't park on a yellow line at all."

"How many parking tickets have you issued this morning?" asked Belinda.

"This is the thirteenth," announced Doris. "What about you?"

10 "Only four," answered Belinda.

Doris laughed scornfully. "The trouble with you is that you're too soft-hearted for this job." She finished writing out the ticket and fixed it onto the windscreen. "Come on," she said, "let's go and have a cup of tea."

15 Doris and Belinda went into Sam's café at the end of the street, and Belinda paid for two teas. Some building workers were sitting at the next table having their dinner.

"Well, girls," said one of them, leaning across, "how many poor motorists did you book this morning?"

20 "Enough," said Doris, without looking up. "Eat your fish and chips and mind your own business."

A   Oral questions

1 Ask what Doris has decided to do about the car.
2 Answer the question.
3 What's Belinda's objection?
4 What did Doris say the driver shouldn't do?
5 Ask how many tickets Doris issued during the morning.
6 Answer the question.
7 Ask how Doris laughed when she learnt that Belinda had only issued four parking tickets.
8 Answer the question.
9 Ask what Doris then suggested.
10 Ask where Doris and Belinda went for their cup of tea.
11 Ask who paid for the teas.
12 Who was sitting at the next table?
13 What question did one of the building workers ask?
14 Ask what Doris told him to do.
15 Answer the question.

UNIT 14 Simple Past v Present Perfect

B   Check that you can remember when to use *since* **and when to use** *for*. **If you have any problems, look at unit 9 again.**

1   Max has lived in the USA _____ thirty years.

2   Emma has worked here _____ 1969.

3   I've been taking these pills _____ two years.

4   He's been smoking _____ he was sixteen.

5   I haven't played football _____ ten years.

6   It's a long time _____ I saw such a good film.

7   She's been on the phone _____ a long time.

8   He hasn't seen her _____ Christmas.

9   I haven't been home _____ a month.

10   It's been there _____ ages.

C   Ask questions using the simple past.

1   Find out when George got his present job.
2   Find out if it rained last night.
3   Find out if our team won the football match.
4   Find out when Emma got home last night.
5   Find out when John bought his new camera.
6   Find out if Toby went to the library yesterday.
7   Find out if Richard bought the record he wanted last week.
8   Find out if they repaired Sid's car yesterday.

D   In conversation we often reply to a PRESENT PERFECT statement with either a *going to* **future or a SIMPLE PAST question, like this:**

I'VE TAKEN THE EXAM.
OH, HOW DID YOU GET ON?

I'VE TAKEN THE EXAM.
WHEN ARE YOU GOING TO GET THE RESULT?

Now reply as naturally as possible in the following situations, using one of these alternatives.

1   I've taken that film to be developed.
2   I've spoken to Mr Harrison about that job.
3   I've ordered the new car.
4   I've got those tickets for the theatre.
5   I've bought a bicycle.
6   Geoff's broken his leg.
7   The television's gone wrong.
8   George has seen the bank manager.
9   John's finished his book.
10   Julie's had the results of those X-rays.

E   Here are some more of the sort of questions you might have to reply to in an ordinary conversation. Try and find interesting replies.

1   Why didn't you phone me last night?
2   Where have you been?
3   Have you had something to eat?
4   What have you been doing since we last met?
5   Did you see that article about Italian gestures in *The Times*?
6   How did you get that black eye?
7   Did you read that book I lent you?
8   Did you get your slides back from Kodak?
9   Why didn't you tell me you were going to be late?
10   What did you do last Sunday?

F   Idea for discussion

Holidays

What is the purpose of a holiday? Is it better to have one four-week holiday, or two two-week holidays? Do you like active holidays, or restful holidays? Has anyone in the class ever been any-where exotic for a holiday? How did you spend your last holiday? Do we find that holidays send us back to work feeling refreshed, or do we too often return to the office needing a week to get over[1] our holiday?

Special points to note

The distinction between the **simple past** and the **present perfect** is different in English from what it is in most other languages, and even when a student is able to explain the difference ration-

[1] get over: recover from

ally, he still sometimes makes mistakes. The student has to learn to *feel* the difference.

Examples:

PETER Have you ever been to Finland?
JOHN Yes, I went there for a holiday in 1975.

Note:

As soon as John senses that he is going to state the time, he automatically switches the conversation to the **simple past**.

MARY Have you applied for that job?
PETER I did, ages ago.

Note:

Peter is defending himself. He wants to express the idea that he did it A LONG TIME AGO, so again he uses the **simple past**.

PETER I've often wondered what it would be like to be a postman. Now I know, because this Christmas I'VE BEEN working as a temporary postman.

Note:

Here no point of time is involved. Peter is obviously speaking during the Christmas holiday.

In order to develop your feeling for the **simple past/present perfect** relationship in English, you should get into the habit of collecting interesting examples and studying them carefully, especially if they surprise you!

**WRITTEN
SECTION**

My Brother

A **Look carefully at this text, then put the verbs into the correct tenses.**

My brother is an interesting chap. For the past two years he (*work 1*) for a big chain of hotels. Before that he (*have 2*) a job with Trans-American Airlines. There was a time when he (*intend 3*) to become a lawyer. He (*start 4*) his training and (*work 5*) for some time for a firm of solicitors. He also (*study 6*) in the evenings. He (*take 7*) the first of his examinations and (*pass 8*). But one day he (*come 9*) home and (*shock 10*) the whole family.
    "I (*decide 11*) to give up law," he (*announce 12*), and he (*do 13*). Recently he (*travel 14*) a lot. During the last couple of years he (*visit 15*) India, Australia, West Africa and South America.

B **Complete the sentences below:**

a) with since _____
b) with for _____

1 I haven't been to the pictures since _____.
                                    for _____.

2 I haven't seen a dentist since _____.
                              for _____.

3 I haven't watched television since _____.
                                  for _____.

4 I haven't looked at a newspaper since _____.
                                     for _____.

5 I haven't spoken a word in my own language since _____.
                                                for _____.

UNIT 14　Simple Past v Present Perfect

C Put the verbs in the sentences below into the correct tense.

1 I (*visit*) Hampton Court six months ago.
2 Hans (*never be*) to Oxford.
3 We (*move*) into our new flat. It's quite comfortable.
4 I'm afraid I (*not finish*) writing that letter yet.
5 That old car (*be*) there since Easter.
6 She (*come*) to London six months ago.
7 I (*not be*) very well last week.
8 Goodness I'm hot. I (*work*) in the garden.

9 I (*live*) here for the last six months.
10 They (*change*) their telephone number last month.
11 When do you (*get*) back to England?
12 I (*not see*) Sally since she was a little girl.

D Composition

Write a composition called "The best holiday I ever had."
Write about a real holiday.

Henry VIII and the Bit of Chair

Some students were visiting Cambridge last week and the guide stopped outside the main entrance to Trinity College.

"Above the gate," he said, "you can see the figure of King Henry VIII, the founder of the College. Can anyone tell me what he is holding in his
5　hand?"

"The orb," said one of the top-class students, "a sort of little world with a cross on top of it!"

"Quite correct," said the guide, "and what is he holding in his other hand?"
10　　"A sword," said someone.

"No, it isn't a sword," said another student, who was looking at his guide book, "it's a sceptre."

"Ah yes," said the guide, "that's what it should be, but look again."

The students looked again. "Why," said one of them, "it's a bit of old
15　chair!"

"Well done," said the guide. "The students here used to think it was very clever to climb up, remove the sceptre from Henry's hand, and

replace it with a bit of chair; then the poor old College porter had to climb up and put it back again. But the College authorities got tired of this game.
20 They said: "Oh well, children will be children," and they left Henry holding his bit of chair. That finished it. Now nobody climbs up there any more."

   "Gracious me," said an old lady who was passing, "I've never noticed that before."

A   Oral questions

1 Ask when the students went to Cambridge.
2 Ask where the students stopped.
3 Answer the question.
4 Ask who told the story.
5 Answer the question.
6 Ask what Henry was holding in his hand.
7 Ask what the College authorities got tired of.
8 Ask if many students climb up there now.
9 Answer the question.
10 What was the old lady doing when she made her remark?

Simple Past v Past Continuous UNIT 15

B   Look at this pattern:

The students/visit Cambridge/guide stop outside
Trinity College.
The students WERE VISITING Cambridge, and the
guide STOPPED outside Trinity College.

The old lady/pass/when/make her remark.
The old lady WAS PASSING, when she MADE her
remark.

*Now use the notes below to make sentences each
containing a* **past continuous/simple past**
combination.

1   The car/overtake the lorry/when skid
2   The people/come out of the cinema/the
    bomb explode
3   Mary/prepare the salad/when cut finger
4   George/play football/injure leg
5   Kevin/play electric guitar/get nasty shock
6   Kathy/bake some cakes/burn hand
7   The lorry/go down hill/when brakes fail
8   The sun/sink in the west/as we walk home
    across fields
9   I/live in Amsterdam/when I meet Barbara
    Wong
10 Tom/write a letter/when Gladys arrive
11 She/ski in Switzerland/when she have the
    accident
12 I/watch a film on the TV/when Henry phone

C   Henry's new car

It was Saturday morning. Mr Jones was working
in the garden. Mrs Jones was washing up in the
kitchen, and their daughter Judy was reading the
paper. Suddenly the door bell rang. Mrs Jones
popped her head round the kitchen door:

"Judy dear, see who it is."

Judy sighed, put down the paper and went to
the front door. Some moments later she returned
with a tall, slim young man in an orange shirt.

"Mum," she said, "Henry's got his new car.
It's lovely. Would you like to come and look at
it?"

Mrs Jones dried her hands, took off her apron,
and called her husband.

"Come and see Henry's new car, dear!"

Mr Jones put down his spade and followed the
others through to the front.

The car was standing outside the house. It was

a long, low, bright yellow two-seater. They all
agreed that it was beautiful.

"Can I go for a little drive with Henry?" asked
Judy.

"All right," said her mother, "but lunch is at
one o'clock, so don't be late!"

Now answer these questions:

1   What was Mr Jones doing?
2   What was Mrs Jones doing?
3   What was Judy doing?
4   What happened to interrupt all these
    activities?
5   What did Judy's mother ask her to do?
6   What three things did Judy do?
7   What did Henry have outside?
8   What did Judy suggest her mother should
    do?
9   What three things did her mother do?
10 What two things did Judy's father do?
11 Where was the car standing?
12 What did they all agree about it?
13 What did Henry want to do?
14 Did Judy's mother agree?
15 What did she remind her daughter?

D   You and the rest of your class are staying at a
beautiful and expensive hotel beside a lake.
Amongst your fellow guests is Prince Ali
Foorooshan, whose wife is the owner of the
famous Kong Diamond, one of the biggest in the
world. The Princess planned to wear the jewel at
dinner this evening, but while she was changing,
it was stolen from her apartment. As soon as she
discovered it was missing, she screamed. The
time she screamed has been established as 7.40
pm; it was on her dressing table at 7.35 pm, so the
police want to know where everyone was, and
what they were doing at that time.

You might have been:

in the bar
in the television room
in the disco
in the dining room
in the library
by the swimming pool
on the lawn in front of the hotel
in your room

UNIT 15   Simple Past v Past Continuous

Get ready to tell the detective:

Where you were.
What you were doing.
What you did when you heard the scream.

E   Idea for discussion

When I was small, I woke up one night, and I was sure I could see a dark figure, standing by the door, looking at me. I lay there, with my heart beating wildly. Then I called my father, and he came and showed me that the 'dark figure' was only my dressing-gown, hanging on the door.

Fear is a funny thing. What sort of things are you afraid of? Are you frightened of spiders, or mice? Have you ever been frightened in a car? In an aeroplane? Do you remember being frightened, when you were a child?

Note how we form the PAST CONTINUOUS:

STATEMENTS	I	was		
	You	were		
	He/she/it	was	passing	when it happened.
	We/you/they	were		

NEGATIVES	I	wasn't		
	You	weren't		
	He/she/it	wasn't	passing	when it happened.
	We/you/they	weren't		

QUESTIONS	Was	I		
	Were	you		before he knocked
	Was	he/she/it	making a noise	on the wall?
	Were	we/you/they		

Special points to note

The **past continuous** is the tense you will use when you want to explain the background to some happening. You will find that you nearly always use it in combination with a **simple past**.

The students WERE PASSING the college, and the guide stopped outside the main gate.

"Gracious me," said an old lady, who WAS PASSING . . .

"What WERE YOU DOING, when I saw you last night?"
"I WAS WAITING for Elizabeth."

Tony WAS OPENING a tin of beans, when he cut his finger.

"Don't speak to me like that!"
"I WASN'T TALKING to you."

The Little Girl and the Lady with the Big Hat

The little girl was sitting on the bus beside her mother. She was wearing a red jumper and a short blue skirt. She was about four years old.

    The bus stopped, and some more passengers got on. They didn't speak. They sat down in the first empty seats they came to, and it was very quiet
5 in the bus.

    The last passenger to come on board was very tall. She was carrying an elegant blue umbrella and an expensive crocodile handbag. She was wearing a very large hat.

    The little girl stared at the hat. "Mummy," she said loudly, "what a
10 funny hat."

    "Shh, dear," said her mother, "don't be so rude."

    Someone at the back of the bus giggled.

    "But it *is* a funny hat," said the little girl defiantly.

    The owner of the hat turned and gave the little girl a frozen smile.

15   "Oh dear, I *am* sorry," said the mother, "children can be so embarrassing."

    All the other passengers smiled happily to themselves.

A Questions on the text

1 Where did this incident take place?
2 Ask what the little girl was wearing.
3 Answer the question.
4 Ask how old the little girl was.
5 Answer the question.
6 Was it noisy in the bus?
7 What was the last passenger to come on board carrying?
8 What was she wearing?
9 How did the little girl look at the hat?
10 What were the exact words she used about it?

B Here are the answers to some more questions about the story. You ask the questions.

1 A small girl.
 Who . . . mother?
2 About four.
 How . . . ?
3 It stopped.
 What . . . do?
4 No, they didn't.
 . . . speak a lot?
5 A blue coat and a large hat.
 What . . . ?
6 The lady's hat.
 What . . . at?
7 Someone at the back of the bus.
 Who . . . ?
8 No, she didn't.
 Did . . . very angry?
9 Very embarrassed.
 How . . . ?
10 They smiled happily to themselves.
 What . . . ?

C Here are ideas for four very short stories. The writer has stated the facts, using only the **SIMPLE PRESENT** tense. Write the stories properly, using past tenses and joining the sentences together where necessary.

1 Tom Black is a famous footballer.
 One day he plays golf.
 Suddenly the sky is filled with black clouds.
 There is a violent thunderstorm.
 Tom shelters under a big tree.
 Lightning strikes the tree.
 Tom is killed.

2 Brenda stops outside the antique shop.
 She looks in the window.
 Suddenly she sees a blue and white vase.
 She likes it very much.
 So she goes into the shop.
 She asks to see the vase.
 The assistant hands it to her.
 She examines it.
 It slips from her fingers.
 It falls to the ground.
 It breaks.
 Brenda feels very embarrassed.
 The assistant says she must pay for it.

3 Christine walks down the road.
 She stops at the bus stop.
 She waits for the bus.
 David comes down the road in his car.
 He sees Christine.
 He stops and offers her a lift.
 "Oh thank you," says Christine.
 He drives her home.

4 Jane watches television.
 Suddenly she feels bored and lonely.
 She gets up.
 She goes to the telephone.
 She rings her friend Joyce.
 Joyce is with a boy called Manuel in a disco.
 So nobody answers the telephone.

D Composition

Write a composition called "The time I was really frightened." Describe something that really happened to you.

Used to . . . **UNIT 16**

An Old Man Remembers

An old man was sitting on a seat in a small park, surrounded by new red brick houses. A young man with a dog came up and sat down beside him.

"It's all changed," said the old man, shaking his head sadly. "You see over there, where those houses are. That used to be the orchard. They

5   used to grow some of the finest pears and apples in the County there.

"And over there; you see that house with the green door; there used to be a pond there. When I was a lad, we often used to fish in it. I don't know what happened to that pond. It must still be there somewhere, under somebody's foundations."

10   "Are you sure it was there?" asked the young man. "Where the house with the green door stands?"

"I'm positive," replied the old man.

The young man looked a little anxious.

"That's my house," he said, "the one with the green door."

A   Oral questions

1   Where was the old man sitting?
2   What was the park surrounded by?
3   "It's all changed," the old man said. What did he do as he said these words?
4   What did the old man say they used to grow in the orchards?
5   What used to be where the house with the green door stands?
6   Where does the old man say the pond must be?
7   What is the old man's reply to the question: "Are you sure it was there?"
8   Why did the young man look anxious?

UNIT 16 Used to . . .

B We can say: They grew fine apples there
or
They *used to* grow fine apples there

Turn the following thoughts into USED TO ideas:

1 They kept cows in that field.
2 There was a tall hedge here.
3 We went to the seaside in the summer.
4 My father took us sailing on the lake.
5 We often went for picnics in the woods.
6 Silvia lived in Kiel, now she lives in Munich.
7 I liked sugar in my tea when I was very young, now I don't.
8 There was a meadow where that school stands.
9 He had his own horses at one time.
10 At one time everybody went to church on a Sunday.

C Study this sentence:

My brother used to work for PanAm, now he works for Intercontinental Hotels.

We often use this combination of *used to* with a **simple present** idea. Make similar sentences:

1 Kim live Georgia/now Texas
2 Alice dancer/now actress
3 Sylvia play guitar/now cello
4 Bob drive long distance lorry/now coach
5 Mr Church repair clocks/now watches
6 Cyril write *The Times*/now the *Telegraph*
7 George play for Spurs/now Fulham
8 Frank teach children/now adults
9 David soldier/now policeman
10 Amelia write love stories/now detective stories

Now what about you? Can you think of some similar statements you could make about yourself?

D Think back to when you were a child. Answer the following questions as truthfully as possible, using *used to*:

Example:
WHERE DID YOU GO TO SCHOOL?

I USED TO GO TO SCHOOL IN LINZ.

1 Give the name of a child you played with when you were young.
2 What sort of food did you like then?
3 What games did you enjoy?
4 What was your favourite season of the year?
5 What sort of thing did you do in the holidays?
6 What did you dislike doing?
7 Where did you live?
8 What toys did you have?
9 How did you go to school?
10 Which lessons did you like?

E The negative form of *used to* is *didn't use to* and to ask questions we use the form: *Did you use to . . . ?*

Look at this conversation:

LOUISE "Did you use to like school?"
SALLY "Yes, I did, didn't you?"
or "No, I didn't, did you?"

Notice how Sally uses the question tag, DIDN'T YOU with the YES answer and DID YOU with the NO answer:

Make more conversations like this. Here are some ideas:

have many friends
like your teachers
enjoy writing compositions
play a lot of games
dislike any lessons

F Idea for discussion

There comes a moment for most children – sometimes a rather awful moment – when they realise that their parents are not perfect. Can you remember any special moment when this happened to you?

As children grow up, they often 'clash' horribly with their parents, and sometimes reach a point where they feel that their parents are wrong about almost everything. Did this happen to you?

What things did you disagree about? Who was right, you or your parents? What was the discipline like in your family? Who could you 'get round' easiest, your Mum or your Dad? Do you think you might have the same problems with your children one day?

Used to . . .

Note how we form the USED TO construction:

STATEMENTS	They	used to	grow	fine apples there.

NEGATIVES	I	used not to / didn't use to	take sugar in my tea.

QUESTIONS	Did	he you they	use to	live in Windsor?

Special points to note

You will find this construction useful when you want to talk about:

a) Anything that happened or didn't happen regularly in the past.

THEY USED TO GO TO CHURCH EVERY SUNDAY.
THAT'S NOT TRUE. THEY DIDN'T USE TO GO EVERY SUNDAY.

b) Things that WERE true, but aren't any more.

DID THERE USE TO BE AN ORCHARD THERE?
YES, THERE USED TO BE AN ORCHARD WHERE THOSE HOUSES STAND.

DIDN'T YOUR BROTHER USE TO LIVE IN FRANCE?
YES, HE USED TO LIVE IN FRANCE, BUT NOW HE LIVES IN SWEDEN.

The negative term of USED TO is DIDN'T USE TO, or USED NOT TO, or NEVER USED TO (which is stronger in meaning).

UNIT 16   Used to . . .

Tiger

We used to have a cat called Tiger. He was a beautiful tabby with a great deal of character. He was a natural hunter, and very soon no mouse dared to show his face in our house.

Unfortunately Tiger also used to catch a lot of birds, and this made him
5 very unpopular with some of the neighbours. One day, just after his second birthday, Tiger disappeared. Perhaps he was run over by a car, for at that time we lived near a busy street. Although we offered a reward, we never discovered what had happened to him, and we never saw him again.

Used to . . .   UNIT 16

A   Do this exercise

1   Ask what pet the writer used to have.
2   What sort of a cat was he?
3   What didn't the mice dare to do, after the arrival of Tiger?
4   Ask what the neighbours thought of Tiger.
5   Answer the question.
6   Why?
7   What happened just after Tiger's second birthday?
8   What may have happened to him? (*Begin*: Perhaps . . .)
9   Where did the writer live at that time?
10   Ask if the writer discovered what happened to Tiger.
11   Answer the question.
12   What did the writer offer in return for information?

B   When I was young, I used to . . .

Write eight sentences describing things you used to do at the weekend, when you were a child.

C   Think of your own country. Imagine you are describing some scene that has changed to a visitor to your country.

Example:

THERE USED TO BE AN OLD CASTLE, WHERE THOSE BUILDINGS STAND TODAY.

Write down five ideas like this, each containing USED TO . . .

D   Composition

Think back to your first year at school. Write a short account of the things you used to do, and the way you used to feel.

UNIT 17 To be / get } used to + -ing

When Frank went to Zürich

Frank worked for a Swiss firm in London. One day the boss called him into his office.

"Frank," he said, "we're sending you to Zürich for a month, to learn about some new equipment."

5 So two weeks later, Frank walked into the Zürich office of the company, and reported to Herr Honig, the Swiss manager.

"Welcome to Zürich," said Herr Honig, "it's nice to have you with us; I'll see you at 7.30 in the morning."

"My goodness," replied Frank, looking rather shocked, "I'm not used
10 to getting up as early as that! In London we start work at 9.00 am."

"What terrible habits," smiled Herr Honig, shaking his head, "but don't worry, you'll soon get used to it." And he was right. Not only did Frank get used to getting up at 6.00 am, but he also got used to drinking coffee at breakfast time instead of tea.

A Oral questions

1 Ask where Frank worked.
2 Answer the question.
3 Where are they going to send him?
4 Why?
5 Ask who welcomed him to the Swiss office.
6 Answer the question.
7 What were the exact words said by Herr Honig that shocked Frank?
8 Why did they shock him?
9 What did Herr Honig say to cheer him up?[1]
10 What did Frank get used to?

[1] cheer him up: make him feel happier

To be | used to + -ing
get |

B Study this idea:

Frank is British. He gets up late.   (*early*)
He isn't used to getting up early.

Now use the ideas below to make similar sentences:

1 Hans comes from Germany. At home he drinks coffee in the morning. (*tea*)
2 Pierre comes from France. In France they drive on the right. (*left*)
3 John usually plays the bass guitar. (*lead guitar*)
4 Christine has always cooked on gas. (*electricity*)
5 Don was brought up on a farm. He lived in the country till he was eighteen. Recently he got a job in the city. (*city*)
6 Elba comes from Maracaibo in Venezuela. It's very hot there. (*a cold climate*)
7 Marc has a car at home. In London he has to travel on public transport. (*public transport*)
8 James married a Japanese girl called Mineko. He went to live in Kyoto. Japanese people eat rice for breakfast. (*rice*)
9 Tony usually gets to bed early. At the business men's conference, the delegates stay up till 1.00 am every night. (*late*)
10 Malcolm went to teach English in Libya. In Libya they eat very strong curry. (*curry*)

C Study this idea:

Frank's British. He gets up late. (*early*)
He soon got used to getting up early.

Use the ideas in exercise **B** to make similar sentences using GOT USED TO + -ING.

D Herr Honig said this:

You will soon get used to it.

Study this idea:

John is going to work in Senegal. He is worried about the heat.

A friend says:

Don't worry. You'll SOON GET USED TO the heat.

Give your friend cheerful, comforting advice in the following situations:

Begin: Don't worry . . .

1 Peter is going to work in Greece. He is worried about the food.
2 Consuela is coming to London. She is worried about the climate.
3 George is going to Saudi Arabia. He is worried because the customs are different from those in Europe.
4 Mary's boss has just introduced a completely new filing system. She finds it confusing.
5 Karla has got a job in the north of Scotland. It always seems to be windy there.
6 Ronald is going to France. He speaks French quite well, but he has never had any practice using French money.
7 Joan has always used an ordinary typewriter. Now her boss has bought an electric machine.
8 Karin is going to work in the north of Germany, in Schleswig-Holstein. She has heard that the people are cold and unfriendly.

E Frank says:

I'm not used to getting up early.

Since Frank has been sent to Zürich he is obviously used to handling equipment of some sort. He could say:

I'm used to handling this type of machine.

Now think of some things *you* are used to doing or aren't used to doing.

F Idea for discussion

Frank had always lived at home with his mother and father in the big, family house, in a London suburb. Then his father retired and bought a bungalow at the seaside. In order to pay for the bungalow, he had to sell the family home. However, he lent George the deposit to buy a small flat. But George soon found there were a lot of things he had to get used to doing for himself.

Talk about them. Begin: He had to get used to . . .

UNIT 17 To be } used to + -ing
get }

Note how we form this construction:

STATEMENT	He	is is getting was got was getting will get is going to get has got	used to	living in France.

NEGATIVES	He	isn't isn't getting didn't get won't get isn't going to get hasn't got	used to	living in France.

QUESTIONS	Is	he	getting going to get	used to	living in France?
	Did Will		get		
	Has		got		

Special points to note

This is a useful way of expressing the ACCUSTOMED TO idea. It can be used with various tenses.

Examples:

I'M NOT USED TO GETTING UP SO EARLY.
YOU'LL SOON GET USED TO IT.
HE SOON GOT USED TO DRINKING COFFEE.
DID YOU GET USED TO LIVING IN SWITZERLAND?

To be } used to + -ing
get }

Conversation at a bus stop

Tom and Jenny wanted to see the film at the Odeon. Tom's car was in the garage for servicing, so they were waiting for the bus. It was cold, and it was raining.

TOM   I'm not used to waiting for buses. I think I'll go and telephone for
5   a mini-cab.

JENNY   Is there a telephone nearby?

TOM   There used to be one in front of those shops.

JENNY   Well, it isn't there now, is it?

TOM   Perhaps they've moved it round the corner. I think I'll go and
10   have a look.

JENNY   You know what'll happen if you go away – the bus will come.

TOM   I won't be a moment.

Tom crossed the road and disappeared round the corner. At that moment the bus came into view. It pulled up at the bus stop and an old
15 lady got off. As it drove away, Tom reappeared.

TOM   Blast. There wasn't a telephone box there after all.

JENNY   I told you that would happen – now we'll have to wait for the next
            one.

A   Questions on the text.

1   Where did Tom and Jenny want to go?
2   Where were they waiting?
3   What was the weather like?
4   What does Tom say about waiting for buses?
5   What does he decide to do?
6   What does Tom say, when Jenny asks if there is a telephone nearby?
7   What does Jenny say will happen if he goes away?
8   Did the bus come?
9   Who got off the bus?
10   Did Tom find a telephone box?

UNIT 17 To be } used to + -ing
get }

B Look at this pattern:

I'm not accustomed to waiting for buses.
I'm not USED TO waiting for buses.

Now turn the ACCUSTOMED TO -ING ideas into USED TO -ING ideas in the following sentences.

1 He isn't accustomed to working with his hands.
2 She isn't accustomed to doing her own housework.
3 He's not accustomed to typing his own letters.
4 He soon got accustomed to getting up at 5.00 am.
5 We're accustomed to living in this country.
6 You'll soon get accustomed to living in a town.
7 He must get accustomed to taking orders.
8 She can't get accustomed to driving on the left hand side of the road.

C In some countries, there is compulsory military service. If you became a soldier, you would have to get used to doing various things. When Terry Francis was called up,

HE GOT USED TO OBEYING ORDERS.

Use the notes below to say what other things he got used to doing.

1 early.
2 clean.
3 food.
4 uniform.
5 sleep.
6 rifle.

D Composition

George Jones used to work at a small, village branch of the bank. There were only two people on the staff, himself and the manager, Mr Hodges. Mr Hodges was in his early sixties and he didn't come in till about ten in the morning. So it didn't matter if George got to the bank a bit late, he didn't have to wear a suit, and everything was very relaxed. If George wanted to go home a bit early, or have the afternoon off for a game of tennis, or a spot of fishing, there were no problems, provided he warned Mr Hodges the day before. Then, one terrible day, the letter came. George was being transferred to the international branch of the bank in the city. Here life was very different . . .

Continue the story.

Mr Polly

One day, you should read *The History of Mr Polly*. It's a good story, and
Mr Polly was one of H G Wells's most memorable characters.

He started his career as an apprentice in a second class department
store. Then his father died and left him a little money.

5   When Mr Polly went to his father's funeral, he had no idea that he was
going to meet his future wife, Miriam. But he did meet her. With the
money his father left him, Mr Polly bought a little shop. But he was a very
unsuccessful business man, and his marriage to Miriam turned out to be a
disaster.

UNIT 18　Future in the Past

10　　He put up with the situation for fifteen years. Then he decided to end it all by setting the shop on fire and cutting his throat while Miriam was at church. He made all his preparations very carefully. He started the fire, but he didn't realise how quickly it was going to spread. Then he remem-

15　bered that there was a deaf, old lady next door, who was going to be burnt to death if he didn't do something immediately. So he dashed upstairs and rescued her. Naturally, he had no time to cut his throat.

　　But life with Miriam was intolerable, so he left home, knowing that she would collect the fire insurance money. Then at last Mr Polly found peace of mind and happiness.

A　Oral questions

1　Why should people read *The History of Mr Polly*?
2　What happened to Mr Polly after he left school?
3　How did he suddenly get some money?
4　Who did he meet at his father's funeral?
5　Ask if he knew at once that she was going to be his wife one day.
6　Answer the question.
7　What did he do, as a result of getting the money?
8　A few years later, he realised that he'd made two mistakes. What were they?
9　What did he decide to do?
10　Where was Miriam going to be while he did these things?
11　Did he start the fire successfully?
12　Why didn't he cut his throat?
13　What money did Miriam get after he left home?
14　And what did Mr Polly find at last?

B   Look at this idea

He didn't realise how quickly the fire was going to spread.

There were other things Mr Polly didn't realise. Use the notes below to make similar sentences. Begin: He didn't realise . . .

1   future wife/funeral
2   very unhappy/with Miriam
3   unsuccessful/business man
4   marriage/disaster
5   so difficult/cut his throat
6   old lady/upstairs

C   Now express ideas about yourself in the same way.

Example:

BUS
I DIDN'T REALISE I WAS GOING TO MISS THE BUS.

1   so ill
2   late
3   so much money
4   you here
5   a visa
6   so many things
7   so many telephone calls
8   Angela here
9   for dinner
10   so long

D   Note this sentence:

HE HAD NO IDEA he was going to meet his future wife.

Whenever we use DIDN'T REALISE, we can replace it with HAD NO IDEA.

Example:
BUS
HE HAD NO IDEA HE WAS GOING TO MISS THE BUS.

Use the ideas in exercise C to make up more sentences.

E   Study this idea:

Pauline says in a surprised tone:

It's raining!
SHE DIDN'T THINK it was going to rain.

Here are some more things Pauline said. Make more sentences beginning: "She didn't think . . ."

1   George is coming!
2   It's snowing!
3   Tom's playing!
4   The police car's stopping outside the house!
5   The radio's working!
6   Bob's cleaning the car!
7   Tony's shaving off his beard!
8   George is giving up his job!

F   We can express negative ideas in a similar way.

Pauline says: "John isn't coming to the party." (then he arrives)

Pauline says: "I THOUGHT YOU WEREN'T COMING to the party!"

Make more sentences like this beginning: "I thought you . . ."

1   At the football match. Tom says: "George isn't playing today." Then George walks into the changing room.
2   At the motor race meeting. John says: "Hank isn't driving today." Then Hank brings his car out onto the circuit.
3   At the horse race meeting. George says: "Graham isn't riding today." Then he sees Graham on a horse.
4   In the pub. Peter says: "John isn't drinking any more." Then John walks in.
5   At the dance. Sylvia says: "Tom and Angela aren't going out together now." Then they walk in, hand in hand.
6   In the store. Margaret says: "Lottie isn't working here any more." Then Lottie walks in.
7   In the library. Jenny says: "Gloria isn't coming in any more—we had a row." Then Gloria walks in.
8   At the gym. Jake says: "Bert isn't training here any more." Then Bert appears.

G   Idea for discussion

Mr Polly got married when he was quite young, and his marriage was not a success. A lot of people get married today, and they find that they have made a mistake.

UNIT 18   Future in the Past

WAS GOING TO

Here are some qualities you might look for in a marriage partner. Put them in order of importance and explain why you have done so.

patience / a sense of humour / a capacity for hard work / education / intelligence / a happy personality / honesty / similar tastes to your own / understanding / money

Note the form of the future in the past:

STATEMENTS	James	had no idea didn't realise didn't know	Sarah was going to come to the party

NEGATIVES	James	thought knew	Emma wasn't going to get the job

QUESTIONS	Did you	have any idea realise think	(that) Gilly was going to get the job?

Special points to note:

You will find this tense useful when you are discussing things that happened and which came as a shock or a surprise to people.

I had no idea she WAS GOING TO PLAY that record.
Did you realise she WAS GOING TO COME to the dance?
I had a feeling he WASN'T GOING TO WIN today.

H G Wells

H G Wells was born in 1866. His energy must have been enormous, for he wrote an astonishing number of books. Many of the later ones were concerned with his idea that mankind would have to create a world state, if it was not to end up by destroying itself.

5 There were novels like *Kipps*, *Love and Mr Lewisham* and *The History of Mr Polly*. The best of these are now recognised as classics. But in addition, this incredible man somehow found the time and inspiration to write the stories forecasting future events that entitle him to be known as the father of science fiction.

10 When *The War in the Air* appeared in 1908, how many people could have foreseen that within thirty years great cities were going to be destroyed by bombs dropped from aeroplanes? *The First Men in the Moon* was published in 1901. How many of those who read it realised that men really *were* going to walk on the moon within their lifetime?

15 And what about *The Time Machine* and *The Invisible Man*? Are we going to wake up one morning and find that here too Wells was forecasting events which were going to come true?

A Do this exercise:

1 Why does the writer believe that Wells had a lot of energy?
2 What was the great ideal that Wells worked for?
3 What did he think would happen if a world state was not created?
4 Give the titles of two of Wells's novels.
5 Was *The History of Mr Polly* science fiction?
6 What happened within thirty years of the publication of *The War in the Air*?
7 Give the titles of two of Wells's science fiction stories.
8 What does the writer suggest we might discover one day?

UNIT 18 Future in the Past

WAS GOING TO

B   Sometimes we express surprise by using an exclamation. We can express the same idea by using the phrase:

I DIDN'T THINK . . .

Look at these examples:

IT RAINED!
I DIDN'T THINK IT WAS GOING TO RAIN.

THEY SOLD ALL THE TICKETS!
I DIDN'T THINK THEY WERE GOING TO SELL ALL THE TICKETS.

Use the ideas below to make similar sentences beginning with:

I DIDN'T THINK . . .

1   The train was late!
2   Anna wrote to me!
3   It snowed!
4   The dentist took my tooth out!
5   The museum was closed!
6   My brother sold his house!
7   They gave me a rise!
8   Georgina got angry about the letter!
9   Pat bought me that record!
10 Tom caught some fish!

C   Look at this idea:

How many of those who read it realised that men really WERE going to walk on the moon within their lifetime?

Use the situations below to ask similar questions:

1   A lot of people saw Charlie Chaplin's first film. He became one of the most famous film stars of all time.
2   A few young people used to watch The Beatles at *The Cavern*. The Beatles later became world famous.
3   A lot of spectators watched the seventeen year old Pelé play for Brazil in the World Cup. He became the greatest player ever to wear a Brazilian jersey.
4   A lot of people were present when Charles I was crowned. Some years later he was executed.
5   A lot of people saw the young Muhammad Ali win the world title. He became one of the greatest champions of all time.

D   Composition

Imagine you are a writer. You intend to write a play about a young romantic girl who was sure she was going to be terribly happy when she got married. In fact her husband turned out to be very lazy and selfish, and her life was very different from what she had imagined.

Compare (a) how she thought life was going to be with (b) how it really was.

Superstitions

Not long ago I was invited out to dinner by a girl called Sally. I had only met Sally twice, and she was very, very beautiful. I was flattered. "She likes me," I thought. But I was in for a disappointment.

"I'm so sorry we asked you at such short notice," she said when I
5 arrived, "but we suddenly realised there were going to be thirteen people at the table, so we just had to find somebody else."

A superstition. Thirteen. The unlucky number. Recently I came upon a little group of worried people, gathered round a man lying on the pavement beside a busy London road. They were waiting for an ambulance,
10 because the man had been knocked down by a passing taxi. Apparently he had stepped off the pavement and into the street, to avoid walking under a ladder.

They say this superstition goes back to the days when the gallows were built on a platform. To get up on to the platform you had to climb a ladder.
15 To pass under the shadow of that ladder was very unlucky . . .

Other superstitions are not so easily explained. To see a black cat in England is lucky. But if you see a black cat in India, it is considered very unlucky. There too, if you are about to set out on a long journey, and someone sneezes, you shouldn't go.

20   Break a mirror – you will have seven years' bad luck. Find a four-leafed clover,[1] you will have good luck. Just crazy superstitions, of course.

I have an African friend. One day he said to me: "If ever an African says to you that he is not superstitious, that man is a liar."

Perhaps that is true of all of us.

A Oral questions

1 What happened to the writer?
2 Ask how many times he'd met Sally.
3 Answer the question.
4 What was Sally like?
5 Why did she apologise, when he arrived?
6 Ask what Sally had realised.
7 Answer the question.
8 What did the writer come across recently?
9 What had happened to the man lying on the pavement?
10 Ask why he'd stepped off the pavement.
11 Answer the question.
12 What were the people waiting for?
13 Where were the gallows usually built?
14 How did you get up there?
15 Is it lucky, or unlucky, to see a black cat in your country?
16 What shouldn't you do in India if someone sneezes?
17 What will happen to you if you break a mirror?
18 What might you find in the grass, that is supposed to bring you good luck?
19 Ask what the writer's African friend told him.
20 Answer the question.

[1] a four leafed clover: most clover plants have three leaves; very rarely a plant has four.

B It was Sunday morning. Richard got up late.

Look at this pattern:

He made a cup of tea.
He had a bath.

AFTER HE'D MADE a cup of tea, HE HAD a bath.

Then he did the following things. Join each pair of ideas, to make sentences like the one above.

1 He had a bath.
2 He got dressed.
3 He rang Angela.
4 He fetched the Sunday papers.
5 He had some breakfast.
6 He read the papers.
7 He went outside, and cleaned the car.
8 He tidied the kitchen.
9 He drove to Angela's house.

C Look at this conversation:

Why did Trudi want to borrow a pen?
Because SHE'D FORGOTTEN hers.

Answer the following questions in a similar way:

1 Why did Oswald very much want to buy some cigarettes?
2 Why did Henry take a taxi home last night, instead of the train?
3 Why was the miserable looking man standing in front of his car at the side of the motorway?
4 Why did James pay some money to the ticket collector, when he came down the train?
5 Why did the tennis player suddenly fall to the ground, holding his leg?
6 Why did the ambulance suddenly roar out into the night, with its siren blaring?
7 Why did the actor suddenly stop speaking in the middle of the play, and look towards the side of the stage?
8 Why did the milk that Mary forgot to put in the fridge last night, look and taste so peculiar this morning?
9 Why did they lift the unfortunate jockey onto a stretcher, and put him, gently, into the ambulance?
10 Why did Fred have to put a new worm on his fish-hook?

D Tom was studying to be a social worker. As part of his training, he was taken to visit a prison by a regular prison visitor. One of the things that surprised him was the fact that most of the prisoners didn't look like the prisoners in a film, or on television. Apart from their uniforms, they looked just like people outside the prison. Afterwards, naturally Tom wanted to ask a lot of questions about the prisoners he'd seen.

"What about that little man you were talking to in the woodwork shop? What had he done?"

Note this pattern:

steal/silver/stately home
"He'd stolen a lot of silver from a stately home."

Use the notes to answer the following questions in a similar way:

1 "What about the little Italian who was talking about the Italian football team?"
   shoot/wife's lover
2 "What about the big, quiet man doing the painting?"
   take part/bank robbery
3 "What about the Jamaican playing the guitar?"
   set fire/factory/because/get sack
4 "What about the tall Cypriot with the moustache?"
   murder/wife
5 "What about the nice little Chinaman carving the boat?"
   try/smuggle/heroin/Hong Kong
6 "What about the very young Englishman with the fair hair?"
   knife/policeman
7 "What about the young Scotsman with ginger hair?"
   hit/old man/over the head/steal/50p
8 "What about the very dark fellow with the moustache?"
   try/hijack/aeroplane
9 "What about the young Irishman with the pale face?"
   steal/lorry/loaded with cigarettes
10 "What about the very old man who gave us the tea?"
   steal/jewellery/store/Bond Street

E   Idea for discussion

Are you superstitious? If so, in what way? What sort of people would you expect to be superstitious? Several superstitions are mentioned in the text. Can you think of some more? How do you think superstitions originate?

Note the form of the PAST PERFECT:

STATEMENTS

When / After	I'd (had) fetched the papers,	I made a pot of tea.

I'd (had) been working for some time,	when there was a knock at the door.

NEGATIVES

He didn't realise till later	that he'd (had) lost his passport.

I hadn't (had not) been waiting long,	when the phone rang.

QUESTIONS

Why had nobody noticed before	that the window was broken?

Where had you been staying,	before you moved into the flat?

Special points to note

Sometimes we want to make statements or ask questions about things that happened in the past, and explain that one thing took place *before* something else. Then we use the **Past Perfect**.

A young woman with fair hair came up to him. "May I speak to you?" she asked.
She looked familiar, but he couldn't place her. Then he remembered.
It was the woman HE HAD SEEN in the museum that morning.

He picked up the telephone and dialled, but the line was dead.
Then he saw why. Someone HAD CUT the wire.

The **Past Perfect** is often used in reported speech:

She told me she HAD NEVER BEEN in London before.

The continuous form of the **Past Perfect** is used for an action that began in the past, and continued through to a more recent point of time in the past.

I'D (HAD) BEEN DRIVING for about half-an-hour, when I noticed a strange smell.

HE'D (HAD) BEEN WORKING for the paper for some years when I first met him.

WRITTEN SECTION

Herbert's Homecoming

Herbert Marshall was a student at Cambridge, but his home town was St Albans. It was August and the family had gone to the seaside. Herbert went to France for his holiday, but he ran out of money, and came home a week earlier than he had expected to.

5 His train didn't get into St Albans until just before midnight. The last bus had gone, so he had to walk home. He let himself into the kitchen, and as he was feeling hot and sticky, he took off his shirt to have a wash.

Suddenly he heard heavy footsteps running up the path. The back door burst open, and he found himself surrounded by policemen. They pushed
10 him into the living-room next door, made him sit down, and began asking him questions.

"What's your name?"

"Where do you live?"

"What's in that case?"

15 "What are you doing here?"

"I live here," said Herbert. "I've been on holiday." But nobody listened to him. They just went on asking questions. Then suddenly one of the policeman said:

"Watch him Frank – we'll go and search the house."

20 They left one tall, very young policeman, to guard him.

"Can I put my shirt on?" asked Herbert.

"No," said the policeman, "stay where you are."

Then the others came back with an older man, a sergeant. He asked the same questions, but he listened to Herbert's answers.

25 "I live here," said Herbert, "and I want to put my shirt on." The sergeant looked at him thoughtfully.

"We'll soon settle this," he said.

He went out and came back with a small, sandy-haired man wearing a shabby, brown dressing-gown. It was Herbert's next-door neighbour. He
30 peered at Herbert intently through thick spectacles.

"Oh yes, Sergeant," he said, "that *is* Mr Marshall." Then he disappeared very quickly. The policemen all looked dreadfully disappointed. They were convinced they had caught a burglar.

"Did he ring you up?" asked Herbert. The police sergeant nodded.

35 "He saw a light and understood your family had all gone away to the seaside."

When they'd all gone, Herbert made himself a cup of coffee.

A   Do this exercise:

1   Where was Herbert studying?
2   Ask where the family had gone.
3   Answer the question.
4   Why did Herbert come home from France earlier than expected?
5   Why did he walk home from the station?

UNIT 19 Past Perfect

6   Why did he decide to have a wash?
7   Who did the heavy footsteps he heard belong to?
8   What did they ask him? (four questions, use *reported speech*)
9   Ask if they listened to his replies.
10 What did one of the policemen suddenly tell Frank to do?
11 What did Herbert ask the young policeman? (*reported speech*)
12 Who did the sergeant go and fetch?
13 Why do you think Herbert's next door neighbour wore thick spectacles?
14 Why were the policemen all so disappointed?
15 When did Herbert make himself a cup of coffee?

B   Note this sentence:

He CAME home a week earlier than he HAD EXPECTED TO.

Now put the verbs in the sentences below into the correct tenses. Be careful! The **simple past** won't always come first.

1   The bus (*go*), so he (*walk*) home.
2   The policemen (*think*) that Herbert just (*pack*) the suitcase.
3   He (*tell*) the policemen, he just (*come*) home from France.
4   When he (*identify*) Herbert, the next door neighbour (*disappear*) very quickly.
5   He (*feel*) very embarrassed because he (*make*) a mistake.
6   The policemen (*be*) very disappointed, because they (*not catch*) a burglar.

C   Read this short text. Then answer the questions below.

I was walking home, and I saw a ladder leaning against the wall of a house. Under the ladder there lay a pot of paint, a paintbrush, and a man with a nasty bump on his head.

1   What had the man been doing?
2   What had he been using?
3   What had happened to the pot of paint?
4   What had happened to the man?
5   Why do you think it happened?

D   Read this short text. Then answer the questions below.

I went into a telephone box and found that the receiver had been smashed, and the coin box had been forced open. There was no money in it.

1   What had happened to the receiver?
2   What had happened to the coin box?
3   What had happened to the money?
4   Ask why someone had done this.
5   Answer the question.

E   Composition.

Write a composition called "I'm not superstitious, but . . ."

Connie

Connie had an American father and an English mother. She was eighteen and she was over in England from the USA with a friend. She was visiting her English grandmother who was ninety-one years old and rather deaf. Fortunately Connie's cousin Julie was there to help.

5	GRANDMOTHER	Well, my dear, what have you been doing with yourself?
	CONNIE	Oh, we've been in London this week. We've seen a lot of interesting things.
	GRANDMOTHER	What did you say? Interesting? What's interesting?
	JULIE	She said they'd seen a lot of interesting things.
10	GRANDMOTHER	They? Who's they?
	CONNIE	I have a girl friend with me.
	JULIE	She has a girl friend with her.
	GRANDMOTHER	Have you been to Windsor Castle?
	CONNIE	Yes, we went to Windsor yesterday.
15	GRANDMOTHER	Speak up. My hearing's not too good.

	JULIE	She said they went to Windsor yesterday.
	CONNIE	And we've been to the British Museum. We saw the Egyptian Mummies.
	GRANDMOTHER	Which museum?
20	JULIE	The British Museum. They saw the Egyptian Mummies.
	CONNIE	Next week we're planning to go to the north of England. We want to visit York and see the Cathedral. We'll send you a postcard.
25	GRANDMOTHER	A postcard? Where?
	JULIE	No, she said they would send you a postcard from York.

A   Oral questions

1 What nationality was Connie's father?
2 Where does she live?
3 Ask if she came over to Europe alone.
4 Answer the question.
5 What problem did her grandmother have?
6 What was the relationship between Connie and Julie?
7 Which famous castle did Connie visit?
8 What did Connie and her friend see at the British Museum?
9 Where are they planning to go next week?
10 What does Connie promise to do?

Reported Speech: I

B   Look at this pattern:

"We've seen a lot of interesting things."
She said they'd seen a lot of interesting things.

Turn these ideas into reported speech in the same way:

1   "We've visited the Tower."
2   "We've seen Trafalgar Square."
3   "We've been to the House of Commons."
4   "We've done some shopping in Oxford Street."
5   "We've taken a lot of photos."
6   "We've bought a few souvenirs."
7   "We've heard Big Ben strike the hour."
8   "We've walked down Charing Cross Road."
9   "We've been for a ride in a London taxi cab."
10   "We've travelled on the underground."

C   Note this pattern:

"We are planning to visit York."
She said they were planning to visit York.

Now turn these ideas into reported speech:

1   "I'm hoping to go to Scotland."
2   "I'm taking a photo of St James's Palace."
3   "I'm buying some postcards."
4   "We're going to the zoo."
5   "She's waiting for a taxi."
6   "I'm booking my tickets at the theatre."
7   "They're coming to Hampton Court."
8   "They're putting up their prices."
9   "I'm eating later."
10   "She's travelling home by air."

D   Note this idea:

"We'll send you a postcard."
She said they'd (they would) send us a postcard.

Turn the following remarks into reported speech.

1   "We'll probably visit the Lake District too."
2   "We'll buy a guide book."
3   "We'll enjoy listening to real northern accents."
4   "We'll try some of the local dishes."
5   "We'll let you know what the prices are like."
6   "We'll visit a woollen mill, if we get the chance."
7   "We'll go to Durham to see the cathedral there too."
8   "I'll telephone you on Monday evening."
9   "I expect we'll see some coal mines."
10   "We'll probably come home on Sunday."

E   Note these ideas:

"Where do you come from?"
She asked where we came from.

"What have you been doing?"
She asked what we'd been doing.

Turn these questions into reported speech.

1   "Where have you been today?"
2   "What do you find specially interesting in London?"
3   "What have you been buying?"
4   "Where do you intend to go tomorrow?"
5   "What do you like about York?"
6   "What have you seen today?"
7   "What do you dislike about England?"
8   "What souvenirs have you bought?"
9   "What do you want to buy for your mother?"
10   "What have you bought for your father?"

F   Idea for discussion

Think of a subject about which there has been much discussion recently: 'Women's Liberation' perhaps. Talk about this with a friend, then change partners, and tell your new partner about your friend's opinions on the subject.

UNIT 20 Reported Speech: I

Note how we form sentences in reported speech.

STATEMENTS	She said She told me	they	were planning to go to York. had seen a lot of interesting things. would send us a card.

NEGATIVES	She said She told me	they	weren't going to Scotland. hadn't been to Cambridge. wouldn't be home late.

QUESTIONS	She asked	what we had seen	at the British Museum.

Special points to note

Whenever we want to tell somebody what another person said, we use **reported speech**.

Two of the commonest reported verbs are:

TO SAY and TO TELL

If the reporting verb is in the present, then we do not change the tenses used in the direct speech.

Example:

"I'm a bit hot."
"What is he saying?"
"He SAYS HE'S a bit hot."

But if the reporting verb is in the **past**, as it often is, then we change present into past:

"We are going to York."
SHE SAID they WERE GOING to York.

"We've seen a lot of interesting things."
SHE SAID THEY'D (they had) SEEN a lot of interesting things.

"Connie's friend is American."
SHE SAID Connie's friend WAS American.

WILL becomes WOULD

"I'll send you a card"
SHE SAID SHE'D (she would) send us a card.

TO TELL is always followed by the person who has been told:

"We are going to York"
SHE TOLD her grandmother they WERE going to York.

"We've seen a lot of interesting things"
SHE TOLD US SHE'D SEEN a lot of interesting things.

The commonest reporting verb for questions is TO ASK

Examples:

WHAT IS HER NAME?
HE ASKED WHAT HER NAME WAS.

WHERE HAVE YOU BEEN?
SHE ASKED WHERE HE HAD BEEN.

WHEN ARE YOU COMING AGAIN?
SHE ASKED WHEN HE WAS COMING AGAIN.

Claude and Anna

Claude and Anna had been to the pictures. Now they were sitting in the bus on their way home.

Suddenly Anna said: "Oh, dear."

"What's the matter?" asked Claude.

5   "I've forgotten my key," replied Anna.

Claude looked at his watch. "Never mind. It isn't late. It's only eleven o'clock."

"But my family¹ always go to bed about 10.30." Anna looked terribly worried.

10   "I know," said Claude. "You can sleep on the sofa in the sitting-room in my home."

They arrived at Claude's home ten minutes later.

Claude's landlady, Mrs Briggs, was still up. She was watching television.

15   "This is Anna," said Claude, "she's forgotten her key, so she's going to sleep on the sofa, if that's OK."

"Very well," said Mrs Briggs. "Has she telephoned her landlady?"

"No, she will be in bed by this time," said Claude.

"All right." Mrs Briggs smiled. "I'll telephone Anna's landlady first

20   thing in the morning."

A   Questions on the text

1   Where had Claude and Anna been?
2   How did they travel home?
3   What did Anna forget to take with her?
4   What time did Anna's family usually go to bed?
5   Where did Claude suggest she could sleep?
6   What was Mrs Briggs doing, when they arrived?
7   Did Mrs Briggs offer to telephone Anna's landlady at once?
8   Ask why she didn't do this.
9   Did Mrs Briggs allow Anna to spend the night on the sofa?
10   When did she telephone Anna's landlady?

¹ my family: foreign students living in England always call the family they are living with "my family."

UNIT 20   Reported Speech: I

B Turn the following remarks into reported speech:

1 I've forgotten my key.
   Anna said . . . .

2 They always go to bed about 10.30.
   She said . . . .

3 You can sleep on the sofa.
   Claude said . . . .

4 It isn't late.
   Claude said . . . .

5 She's forgotten her key.
   He said . . . .

6 She's going to sleep on the sofa.
   He said . . . .

7 It's only eleven o'clock.
   He said . . . .

8 She will be in bed by this time.
   He said . . . .

9 That's all right.
   She said . . . .

10 I'll telephone in the morning.
    She said . . . .

C Note again how we turn questions into reported speech.

"What have you eaten today?"
Mrs Briggs asked what they had eaten that day.

Turn these questions into reported speech in the same way:

1 "Where does Anna come from?"
   Mrs Briggs asked . . . .

2 "What has Anna forgotten?"
   Mrs Briggs asked . . . .

3 "Can you give me your landlady's telephone number?"
   Mrs Briggs asked . . . .

4 "Where can I sleep?"
   Anna asked . . . .

5 "What time does your landlady go to bed?"
   Mrs Briggs asked . . . .

D Composition

The electricity workers are on strike for more money. Mr Crump, a representative of the electricity workers' union, is being interviewed on TV by Dan Fergus.

DAN FERGUS   Now you've heard what these members of the general public have to say. This strike of yours is causing great inconvenience to many people. Don't you feel bad about this?

MR CRUMP   Of course we feel bad about it. The last thing we want is to cause inconvenience to the general public. Our quarrel is not with the general public, it is with the employers and the Government.

DAN FERGUS   But the Government have fixed a limit of five per cent on the increase in wages that an employer may offer.

MR CRUMP   Look, two years ago the Government set up a commission to enquire into the wages paid in the electricity industry. That commission recommended a fifteen per cent increase right across the board.[1] Since then we have had inflation at the rate of more than twelve per cent. During that time the electricity worker's pay has increased by an average of six per cent. Do you think that is fair?*

DAN FERGUS   And how long do you anticipate that the strike is going to last?

MR CRUMP   Our members are determined to fight for a fair settlement. All we are asking for is a fair day's pay for a fair day's work. And our members will remain on strike until the Government sees sense.

Imagine you are a journalist. It is your job to make a summary of Mr Crump's remarks. You will, of course, use reported speech.

---

[1] right across the board: for everybody.
* Do you think that is fair?
In reported speech this will become:
He asked if Mr Fergus thought that was fair.

Reported Speech: II

George

George's mother was worried about him. One evening, when her husband came home, she spoke to him about it.

"Look dear," she said, "you *must* talk to George. He left school three months ago. He still hasn't got a job, and he isn't trying to find one. All he
5 does is smoke, eat and play records."

George's father sighed. It had been a very tiring day at the office.

"All right," he said, "I'll talk to him."

"George," said George's mother, knocking at George's door, "your father wants to speak to you."
10 "Oh!"

"Come into the sitting-room dear."

"Hullo old man," said George's father, when George and his mother joined him in the sitting-room.

"Your father's very worried about you," said George's mother. "It's
15 time you found a job."

"Yes," replied George without enthusiasm.

George's mother looked at her husband.

"Any ideas?" he asked hopefully.

"Not really," said George.
20 "What about a job in a bank?" suggested George's mother, "or an insurance company perhaps?"

"I don't want an office job," said George.

George's father nodded sympathetically.

"Well, what *do* you want to do?" asked George's mother.
25 "I'd like to travel," said George.

"Do you want a job with a travel firm then?"

"The trouble is," said George, "I don't really *want* a job at the moment. I'd just like to travel and see a bit of the world."

George's mother raised her eyes to the ceiling. "I give up," she said.

A Oral questions

1 Why was George's mother worried about him?
2 What did she tell her husband to do?
3 Why did he sigh?
4 What jobs did George's mother suggest he might get?
5 What did George really want to do?

UNIT 21   Reported Speech: II

B   Look at this idea

"Come into the sitting-room."
She told (asked) him to come into the sitting-room.

This is how we tell other people about orders or requests. Deal with the orders or requests below in the same way. Use <u>tell</u> *for an order and* <u>ask</u> *for a request.*

1   "Sit down by the window."
2   "Ring me this evening."
3   "Look in the cupboard."
4   "Take a couple of aspirins."
5   "Pour yourself another whisky."
6   "Ask at the station."
7   "Have another piece of cake."
8   "Write to Head Office about it."
9   "Take it back to the shop where you bought it."
10 "Explain to them what happened."

C   Note this idea:

"You must talk to George."
She said he had to talk to George.

A logical case can be made out for leaving *must* in the present, but it is usually best to follow the *present to past* pattern. This pattern must be followed for the auxiliaries, *can*, *want*, *may*.

"I don't want an office job."
He said he didn't want an office job.

"I can ring the Bank Manager."
He said he could ring the Bank Manager.

"I may go abroad."
He said he might go abroad.

Turn these remarks into reported speech:

1   "I don't want to work in a bank."
2   "I may buy a new one."
3   "I can't just walk in."
4   "I must think about it."
5   "I want the A – D telephone book."
6   "I can't find that address."
7   "I may not be able to ring you this evening."
8   "I can get one on the way home."
9   "I can't do anything about it tonight."
10 "I must contact Brenda today."

D   Look at this question

"What do you want to do?"
She asked what he wanted to do.

Turn the following questions into reported speech:

1   "Where do you want to go?"
2   "Where do you intend to live?"
3   "Why don't you learn Spanish?"
4   "What do you think is going to happen to you?"
5   "Why don't you try and get a job in a bank?"
6   "Where are you going for your holiday?"
7   "Why do you want to go to Greece?"
8   "How do you expect to raise the fare?"
9   "Why don't you get a job as a Courier?"
10 "What do you want to become eventually?"

E   Here is a different sort of question

"Do you want a job with a travel firm?"
She asked if he wanted a job with a travel firm.

Turn these questions into reported speech:

1   "Do you want to go abroad?"
2   "Do you think it will be possible to get a job abroad?"
3   "Do you intend to go to Greece?"
4   "Are you going to answer any advertisements?"
5   "Is there a chance you might continue with your studies?"
6   "Is John trying to get a job?"
7   "Have you been to the Labour Exchange?"
8   "Aren't you tired of doing nothing?"
9   "Haven't you got any plans at all?"
10 "Are you definitely going to leave home?"

F   Revision exercise.

Turn the following statements into reported speech:

1   "You must talk to George."
    She said . . .

2   "He left school three months ago."
    She said . . .

3   "He still hasn't got a job."
    She said . . .

4   "He isn't trying to find a job."
    She said . . .

5 "I'll talk to him."
   He said . . .

6 "Your father wants to speak to you."
   She said . . .

7 "Come into the sitting-room."
   She told . . .

8 "Your father's very worried about you."
   She said . . .

9 "It's time you found a job."
   She told . . .

10 "Have you any ideas?"
   His father asked . . .

11 "I don't want an office job."
   George said . . .

12 "I don't really want a job."
   He said . . .

G Idea for discussion

Here is a list of jobs for boys and girls:

Jobs for boys	*Jobs for girls*
Railway porter	Hairdresser
Waiter	Waitress
Bus driver	Cinema usherette
Bus conductor	Shop assistant
Lorry driver	Post office clerk
Taxi driver	Teacher
Hotel cook	Chocolate factory worker
Policeman	Typist
Shop assistant	Cloak room attendant
Postman	Nurse

Each member of the class must choose one, and the other members of the class must try and persuade him or her that it isn't a nice job. He or she must defend his choice.

Note these new patterns:

STATEMENTS	She asked / She told	me		to come	into the sitting-room.

NEGATIVES	She asked / She told	me	not	to come	into the sitting-room

QUESTIONS WITH 'IF'	She asked	if	he	liked / was leaving / would be in	Prague . . .

Special points to note

You will need to be able to turn orders and requests into reported speech. This is how you do it:

"Come into the sitting-room."

We can say:

She ASKED HIM TO COME into the sitting-room.
She TOLD HIM TO COME into the sitting-room.
She INVITED HIM TO COME into the sitting-room.
She REQUESTED HIM TO COME into the sitting-room.

UNIT 21   Reported Speech: II

Note how we turn questions into reported speech:

"Do you want a job in a bank?"
She ASKED IF HE WANTED a job in a bank.

"Are you going back tonight?"
She ASKED IF HE WAS GOING BACK tonight.

"Will you be in Prague next week?"
She ASKED IF I WOULD BE in Prague this week.
(next week)

Auxiliaries like MUST, CAN usually change into the past.

"You must stay here till Christmas."
He SAID I HAD TO STAY here till Christmas.

"I can't find that address."
He SAID HE COULDN'T FIND that address.

Note one other point:

The **simple past** is sometimes changed into the **past perfect,** but quite often we leave it in the **simple past** when we use a past adverb.

"The letter from the insurance company arrived yesterday."
She told me the letter from the insurance company arrived yesterday.
or
She told me the letter from the insurance company had arrived.

WRITTEN SECTION

Only Going as far as Camberwell

November in London. It was cold and wet and rather foggy. The people in the queue for the 185 bus were getting impatient.

"I've been waiting nearly an hour," said a stout lady with two heavy shopping bags, "and I've got to get home to get the children's tea."

5   "I know," said a tall lady in a green coat, "it's terrible, isn't it?"

"Well, that's your London Transport," said an elderly man irritably. "That's your London Transport." He looked round for approval and the people near him nodded.

At last the bus came. The windows were all steamed up and it was nearly

10   full. As it drew in to the kerb, the conductor leaned out and shouted: "Two only." The first two in the queue climbed aboard and the bus drove off.

"If I see an inspector, I'll give him a piece of my mind," said the stout lady.

"If I were an inspector, I'd keep well out of your way," said a young man

15   in a blue raincoat. He smiled at his pretty pale-faced girl-friend beside him.

"I think it's disgusting," said the stout lady.

Then another bus came. This one was nearly empty and most of the queue were able to get on.

The conductor came to collect the fares. "Forest Hill," said the stout

20   lady.

"Only going as far as Camberwell," said the conductor.

"Do you know I've been waiting over an hour for this bus," said the stout lady angrily.

"Can't help that," said the conductor.

25   "It says Catford on the front," said the elderly man.

"No it doesn't," said the conductor, "it says Camberwell."

At the next stop the conductor got out and went to have a look. He spoke to the driver and the driver changed the sign on the front. When the conductor got in again, the elderly man said triumphantly:

30   "It *did* have Catford on the front!"

"That's not my fault," said the conductor. "I'm only the conductor."

"London Transport!" said the elderly man sarcastically.

At Camberwell all the passengers had to get off and take their places in another queue. They lined up with a sort of patient resignation.

35   "If the bus doesn't come soon, we'll take a taxi," whispered the young man to his girl-friend.

But of course a bus came eventually, and in the end everyone got home to his tea.

A   Do this exercise

1   What was the weather like?
2   Why were the people in the queue annoyed?
3   Why were most of the people able to get on the second bus?
4   What was the argument about between the conductor and a passenger?
5   Who was right?
6   What happened to the passengers at Camberwell?
7   What did the young man decide to do if the bus didn't come soon?
8   Ask if the bus came in the end.

B   Turn the following remarks into reported speech:

1   "I've been waiting for nearly an hour."
The lady said . . .

2   "I've got to get home."
She said . . .

3   "It's terrible."
The second lady said . . .

4   "If I see an inspector, I'll give him a piece of my mind."
The stout lady said that if . . .

5   "I think it's disgusting."
She said . . .

6   "We're only going as far as Camberwell."
The conductor said . . .

7   "Do you know I've been waiting over an hour?"
The stout lady asked . . .

8   "I can't help that."
The conductor said . . .

9   "It says Catford on the front."
The elderly man told . . .

10   "It doesn't, it says Camberwell."
The conductor replied that . . .

C   Peter had an interview for a job with a travel agency. Below are some of the questions he was asked. That evening he discussed the interview with his friend Tom. What did Peter say? Begin each sentence with: He asked me . . .

1   When did you leave school?
2   Where did you go to school?
3   What examinations did you pass?
4   Do you like travelling?
5   Have you spent much time abroad?
6   What foreign languages do you speak?
7   Is your Spanish really fluent?
8   Are you prepared to work hard?
9   Do you mind working at the weekend?
10   Can you keep cool under pressure?

D   Composition

Read the following text carefully:

The man who interviewed Peter (see question **C**) was called Mr Daniels. After the interview he discussed Peter with his chief, Mr Thompson.

Mr Thompson asked Mr Daniels about Peter and Mr Daniels said he was a very pleasant young man. He said he was inexperienced, but had done quite well at school and spoke some French and Spanish.

Mr Thompson asked if Mr Daniels thought Peter could learn the job reasonably quickly and Mr Daniels replied that he seemed very keen and intelligent.

Mr Thompson asked if Mr Daniels had mentioned a specific salary, and Mr Daniels said that he had explained that the starting salary would be quite small, but that it would increase considerably after six months, if Peter proved the right man for the job.

Mr Thompson told Mr Daniels to write and offer Peter a job at a starting salary of £30 a week. Mr Daniels thanked him and promised to do so right away.

Now, using the ideas in the passage, write the dialogue between Mr Daniels and Mr Thompson.

IF YOU GO DOWN THIS ROAD YOU'LL . . .

A Problem With Petrol

Terry had a nice new sports car. The first Sunday after he bought it, he took his girl-friend Muriel for a drive in the country; but unfortunately he thought there was more petrol in the tank than there was – and he ran out of petrol.

5   An old farm hand came down the road towards them, and Terry stopped him.

TERRY	Excuse me, do you know if there's a petrol station near here?
OLD FARM HAND	Have you run out of petrol then?
10 TERRY	Yes.
OLD FARM HAND	Well . . . I can't say there's a petrol station near here.
TERRY	Can you tell me where there is one?
OLD FARM HAND	Well . . . if you go down this road for about half a mile, you'll come to a farm.
15 TERRY	Yes.
OLD FARM HAND	Then you keep straight on, past the farm, till you come to The King's Head.
TERRY	That's a pub.
OLD FARM HAND	You know it then?
20 TERRY	No, no, I just assumed it was a pub. Is the petrol station near there?
OLD FARM HAND	Well . . . no . . . but if you turn right, and go on for about a mile you'll find a garage on the right hand side.
TERRY	I see.
25 OLD FARM HAND	There is one problem though.
TERRY	What's that?
OLD FARM HAND	It's closed on a Sunday.
TERRY	Well, is there a telephone anywhere?
OLD FARM HAND	If I were you, I should ask at the farm.
30 TERRY	All right, thank you.
OLD FARM HAND	You'll have to remember to put enough petrol in the tank next time, won't you?

A   **Oral questions**

1 What did Terry have?
2 Ask what he did, the first Sunday after he bought it.
3 Answer the question.
4 What happened to Terry that probably annoyed him?
5 Ask who he stopped.
6 Answer the question.
7 What did Terry want to know?
8 Did Terry know The King's Head?
9 What was the problem concerning the garage a mile past The King's Head?
10 What did the old farm hand advise him to do next time?

B   Look at this pattern:

"Oh, dear, I look a mess."
make-up/better
"If you put on some make-up, you'll look better."

Use the notes to respond to the following remarks in a similar way:

1   "Oh, dear, I've got a very bad tooth."
dentist/out
2   "Oh, dear, it's a very long journey by bus."
train/quicker
3   "Oh, dear, I'm broke again."
job/money
4   "Oh, dear, my record player has gone wrong again."
save up/new
5   "Oh, dear, I've had a pain in my side for days."
doctor/medicine
6   "Oh, dear, my car won't start."
petrol/will
7   "Oh, dear, I have no idea what the hotel will be like."
write/brochure
8   "Oh, dear, I've had a headache all day."
aspirin/better
9   "Oh, dear, nobody ever writes to me."
write/get
10   "Oh, dear, I can't get a decent picture on my television."
aerial/all right

C   Naturally we can use negatives in similar sentences.

"If we don't get some petrol soon, we shall be in trouble."

Use the ideas below to make more sentences:

1   Kevin hasn't paid his electricity bill. His friend Fred is worried because in cases like that the electricity board sometimes turn off the electricity.
2   Richard's mother wants him to go to bed, but Richard is doing his homework. He is worried about getting into trouble.

3   Tom hasn't arrived yet. You're thinking of going without him.
4   You're fishing. The fish aren't biting. You're thinking of going home.
5   Jenny's little sister has been missing for two hours. She's thinking of ringing the police.
6   The bank robber is talking to the bank clerk. He wants the money. He's thinking of filling the bank clerk full of holes.
7   Mrs Morris is angry with Mr Morris because he still hasn't repaired the fence. She's thinking of getting a builder to do it.
8   Mr Cox is looking at the apple tree. It hasn't had any apples on it for five years. He's only going to give it one more year.
9   The doctor is telling Mr Morris he must cut down on his food. He's afraid he's going to have a heart attack.
10   The referee is annoyed because Parker keeps arguing with his decisions. "Stop arguing," he says. He's thinking of sending him off.

D   Note how we can use *unless* instead of the *if . . . not* idea.

"Unless we get some petrol soon, we shall be in trouble."

Use the situations in **C** to make sentences with UNLESS.

E   We use *if* sentences when we are not sure whether something is going to happen or not. But sometimes we make similar sentences with *when*. In this case, of course, we *know* what is going to happen. Look at this idea:

"What will you do when winter comes?"
"I'll try and get another job."

Now think yourself into the part of the character in question in the following situations, and answer as naturally as possible.

1   (You are a bank robber in prison)
"What will you do when you get out?"
2   (You are a schoolboy)
"What will you do when you leave school?"

IF YOU GO DOWN THIS ROAD YOU'LL . . .

3 (You are a professional footballer)
"What will you do when you retire?"

4 (You are a secretary in a big office. You
recently got engaged)
"What will you do when you are married?"

5 (You are a famous actor, and for the last six
months you have been working on a very long
film)
"What will you do when the film is finished?"

6 (You are a bank clerk who hates his job, and
has decided to give it up)
"What will you do when you leave the bank?"

7 (You are the owner of a big house in the
country that you have decided to sell)
"What will you do when the house is sold?"

8 (You are a waitress in a cheap café, and you
have just won £20,000 on the football pools)
"What will you do when you get the money?"

9 (You are a television actor in a long-running
series)
"What will you do when the programme
ends?"

10 (You are the pilot of a Jumbo Jet airliner)
"What will you do when you get too old to fly
Jumbo Jets?"

*Use the ideas below to make similar sentences using
whenever:*

1 Mike always has to work late when his boss is
away.

2 Dolly gets cross when James comes home
from work late.

3 Josephina always cries when she sees a sad
film.

4 Dolly always wants to watch old Paul
Newman films when they're shown on
television.

5 Josephina always grumbles at Mike when
there are problems with the car.

6 Dolly always makes sandwiches for James
when he goes on a journey.

7 Mike always gets jealous when Josephine
dances with other men.

8 James always feels sleepy when it's time to get
up.

9 Josephina always says Mike is getting too fat
when he asks for another piece of cake.

10 Mike always wants to own Degas sketches
when he sees them.

F Read this conversation

Mike has just come home from work.

JOSEPHINA	What's wrong dear?
MIKE	Nothing.
JOSEPHINA	You're worried about something.
MIKE	I'm not.
JOSEPHINA	Oh, yes, you are. Whenever you start whistling like that, I know something's wrong.
MIKE	Well, I had a bit of an argument with the assistant manager.

Note this idea:

Josephina always knows something's wrong when
Mike starts whistling like that.
Whenever he starts whistling like that, Josephine
knows something's wrong.

G Idea for discussion.

Imagine you are part of a committee responsible
for designing a television programme for a very
small country that has not had its own TV programme before. You can decide where this country will be.

The programme times are limited: 7.00 pm –
10.30 pm every evening, with no advertisements.

Draw up a plan for yourselves like the one on
page 128, and work out a suitable pattern of
programmes for the week.

Useful phrases:

If we put the play on a bit later . . .
How about having . . .
Why not have . . .
I think/don't think we ought to have . . .

UNIT 22 First Conditional:

IF YOU GO DOWN THIS ROAD YOU'LL . . .

Times	Sunday	Monday	Tuesday	Wednesday	Thursday	Friday	Saturday
7.00–							
10.30	Close-down						

Some programme ideas:

For Children
The News
News of the Week
Play of the Week
Detective Story

Love Story
Comedy Hour
Sport
Concert Hour
The Cowboys Ride Again

Note how we form FIRST CONDITIONAL and *whenever* sentences:

STATEMENTS

If	Tom	brings	the car,	we'll	go	to the seaside.

NEGATIVES

If	Tom	doesn't bring	the car,	we	won't go to the seaside.

QUESTIONS

Shall	we	go	to the seaside,	if when	Tom	brings	the car?

Will	you	get	some stamps,	if	you	go	near the post office?

NOTE ALSO

If	it doesn't rain, the weather is nice,	we	can may might	go	to the seaside.

Note also the WHENEVER pattern:

Whenever we go to the seaside, Tom loses something.

128

First Conditional:

UNIT 22

IF YOU GO DOWN THIS ROAD YOU'LL . . .

Special points to note

You will need this construction to talk about things which may or may not happen, depending on something else.

Examples:

"I'LL BUY a new car IF I CAN GET a reasonable price for the old one."

"Our team WILL NEVER SCORE IF THEY GO ON PLAYING like this."

"WILL YOU COME to the Mozart concert IF I BUY the tickets?"

"SHE WON'T MARRY me UNLESS* I GO TO LIVE in Argentina."

WHENEVER means EVERY TIME

Examples:

"WHENEVER I SEE pictures of Japan, I WANT TO go there."

"WHENEVER I SMELL that glue, IT REMINDS me of the model aeroplanes I used to make."

Note that WHENEVER is also used with the **past**.

"WHENEVER HE HEARD that tune, HE THOUGHT of Simone."

* unless: if . . . not.

129

UNIT 22 First Conditional:

IF YOU GO DOWN THIS ROAD YOU'LL . . .

The China Lady

It was twenty past six on Saturday evening when Tom Carter remembered that it was his wife's birthday the next day. All the shops were closed.

"Blast," muttered Tom to himself. Then suddenly he noticed that the antique shop across the road was still open. In the window there was a 5 porcelain figure of a lady, seated at her dressing-table. It was old, slightly damaged and very dusty.

"How much?" asked Tom.

"A fiver," said the dealer.

"Five pounds for that!"

10 "It's a genuine antique."

"I'm looking for a birthday present for my wife," said Tom.

"I'll tell you what," said the dealer, "if she doesn't like it, I'll exchange it."

15 Tom's wife received her present without enthusiasm. "It's filthy," she said.

"If you don't like it," said Tom, "you can take it back and change it." So she took it back to the shop.

"What a lot of old junk," she thought. Then she saw a pair of brass candlesticks.

20 "How much are these?"

"£4.50," said the dealer, hastily adding a pound to the price he had expected them to fetch. So Tom's wife gave the dealer back the china lady, and he gave her the candlesticks and 50p change.

She took the candlesticks home, washed and polished them and put them
25 on the sideboard. Meanwhile the dealer had a good look at the china figure. "I wonder . . ." he said to himself.

A few days later a small piece appeared in the local paper.

ANTIQUE DEALER'S FIND

A local antique dealer, Mr Harry Cox, recently bought a porcelain figure. He sold it for £5, but it was returned by the customer. He then took it to Sotheby's to be valued and it has been identified as an original Meissen piece. It will come up for auction at Sotheby's next Thursday and is expected to fetch at least £3,000.

"Blast!" said Tom when he saw it, "blast, blast and blast."

A   Answer these questions:

1   What was it that Tom suddenly remembered?
2   Which shop was still open?
3   What did he see in the window?
4   What sort of a condition was it in?
5   How much did the dealer want for it?
6   What did the dealer promise to do, if Tom's wife didn't like it?
7   Was Tom's wife very pleased with it?
8   What did she do with it?
9   What did she think about the goods being offered for sale in the antique shop?
10   What did she finally exchange the figure for?
11   What did she do with the candlesticks, when she got them home?
12   Where did the dealer take the figure?
13   Why did he take it there?
14   What is going to happen to it?
15   How much is it expected to fetch?

UNIT 22   First Conditional:

IF YOU GO DOWN THIS ROAD YOU'LL . . .

B   Look at what the dealer said:

"If she doesn't like it, I'll exchange it."

Later he might have said this:

"If it's worth a lot of money, I'll sell it at the auction."

Use the notes below to make similar sentences:

1   If the taxi (*not come*) soon/I (*walk*) to the station.
2   If you (*bring*) the letter to me/I (*type*) it for you.
3   If the party (*go on*) very late/I (*give*) you a lift home.
4   If you (*buy*) that old car/you (*have*) trouble with it.
5   If you (*take*) too much of that medicine/you (*feel*) very sleepy tomorrow.
6   If I (*not ring*) you tomorrow morning/I (*ring*) you in the evening.
7   If you (*not get*) that French cheese from the local shop/you (*get*) it at the supermarket.
8   If you (*order*) that record/it (*be*) here in a few days.
9   If those slides (*not come back*) by the weekend/I (*write*) about them.
10 If the bus (*not come*) soon/I (*go*) by train.

C   Finish each of the sentences below so that it means the same as the sentence printed before it:

1   I always think of Julie when I hear that song.
    Whenever . . .
2   The journey from here to Oxford will take you two hours.
    If you leave at 11 o'clock . . .

3   In Wales the Welsh language can be heard.
    If you go to Wales . . .
4   I always visit the Louvre when I go to Paris.
    Whenever . . .
5   There are a lot of interesting things to see in Edinburgh.
    If you visit . . .
6   People who don't take enough exercise become fat and lazy.
    If you don't . . .

D   Composition

James and Dolly haven't been married long. They live in a small, rented flat in the city, not far from the office where James works. They are thinking of getting a mortgage and buying a house in the suburbs. There are advantages and disadvantages of course.

Advantages	*Disadvantages*
Security of own home	Shortage of money
Freedom to do what they want	No holidays abroad
More space	No new car
Nearer the country	No colour television
Quieter	Longer journey to work for James
A garden	Leave home earlier
Grow their own vegetables	Get home later
Walks in the country	

Write a conversation between Dolly and James, mentioning the points above, and any more you can think of. End by making a decision.

St Martin's Church

The coach drew into the coach park at Canterbury and the students prepared to get out.

"One moment," said the guide. "I know you all want to see the Cathedral, but first I'm going to show you something else."

5   The party followed him past the prison to St Martin's Church. They went inside and he continued quietly:

"St Martin's is probably the oldest church in England where regular Sunday services are still held. We believe it was built during the Roman occupation of Britain, and we know that St Martin's was already standing
10   when St Augustine arrived in AD 597.

"In a moment I want you all to look carefully at the font, where babies are baptised. It is unique. The lower part is Saxon work and you will see that it is decorated with a pattern of circles similar to the motif used for the Olympic

15 Games. The Normans wanted a taller font, so they added the middle bit, but they decorated it in the style that was fashionable at that time.

"Just think," he went on, "how many prayers have been said in this little church during the last fourteen hundred years."

A   Oral questions

1 Ask where the students went.
2 Answer the question.
3 Ask what the students passed on the way to St Martin's.
4 Answer the question.
5 When is it thought that St Martin's was built?
6 Who came to Britain in AD 597?
7 What did the guide ask the students to look at?
8 What happens to babies there?
9 What two styles of decoration can be found on it?
10 What did the guide remark on at the end of his talk?

B   Look carefully at this idea:

The priest baptises babies in the font.
Babies are baptised in the font.

They decorate it with circles.
It is decorated with circles.

*Now change the ideas below into the **passive** in the same way:*

1 They use old bricks to repair the walls.
2 They keep the holy water in here.
3 They hold a service here every Sunday.
4 An old man cuts the grass.
5 Visitors to the church usually put money in that box.
6 You can see the Cathedral from the top of the hill in the churchyard.
7 They bury people in the churchyard.
8 A retired schoolmaster trains the choir.
9 People from all over the world visit the church.
10 You can see some interesting tombstones in the churchyard.

C   Note these ideas

The Romans built the first church.
The first church was built by the Romans.

They made many fine roads in the first century AD.
Many fine roads were made in the first century AD.

*Use the ideas below to make similar **passive** sentences in the past.*

1 The Romans conquered much of southern England.
2 They sent a number of Roman legions to Britain.
3 The Romans built the great defensive wall in the north of England.
4 They built it to defend England against the Scots.
5 The Romans worshipped various different gods.
6 The Romans brought their system of law to Britain.
7 They took many British slaves back to Rome.
8 Queen Boadicea attacked the Romans at Colchester.
9 Eventually the Romans defeated her army.
10 The Romans occupied Britain for about four hundred years.

D Here is a thought:

Just think how many prayers have been said in this little church . . .

There are many situations where we might wish to make remarks like this in a classroom, perhaps we might say:

Just think how many lessons	have been taught	in this room.

Just think how many ——	have been ——	in at this —— on

What might we say:

1 In a concert hall.
2 In a big bank.
3 In an old theatre.
4 In a famous football stadium.
5 At a race track.
6 In a recording studio.
7 In a shoe shop.
8 In the kitchen of a big hotel.
9 Looking at an old violin.
10 Looking at an old office typewriter.

E It is often useful to be able to ask questions using the PASSIVE.

Look at these examples:

You are in a shop looking at a brass ashtray. You want to know if it is Indian.

WAS THIS MADE IN INDIA?

You are about to fix a new cable for the light. You want to make sure the electricity isn't still on.

HAS THE ELECTRICITY BEEN TURNED OFF?

*Make two sentences for each of the following situations, one **active** and one **passive**.*

1 You work in the local library. A man borrowed a rather expensive bird book. You want to know if he has brought it back.

2 You visit a friend's house and notice some beautiful candles. You want to know if he bought them in Germany.

3 You hear a very fine recording. You want to know if they recorded it in the States.

4 You work in a big store. Somebody brings back a tape recorder they claim is faulty. You want to know if they bought it in your store.

5 You are a customs man. Someone has an expensive camera. You want to know if he bought it abroad.

6 You work for the railway company. You have no record of some reservations that someone says he made. You want to know where he made them.

7 You are a clerk dealing with immigration matters. A foreigner says he sent his passport to his embassy. You want to know when.

8 You have a friend who is a freelance journalist. He wrote an article you found very interesting. You want to know if anyone has published it.

9 You want to go to a concert very much. You are afraid they have probably sold all the tickets already. Ask at the box office.

10 Someone stole a typewriter from the office. You want to know if the staff saw anyone leaving the premises with a typewriter under his arm.

F Extract from a letter:

I have sad news. My Lotus sports car, which I have had for more than ten years, has been stolen and vandalised. I'm sure it must have been taken for spare parts because it was found two days ago, abandoned on a building site in Peckham. The engine, the headlamps and the number plates had been removed.

As it is a fairly old model, it is very difficult to get spares. I'm afraid it's going to cost a terrible lot to be repaired, even if the parts can be obtained. I suppose I shall have to start visiting breaker's yards . . .

UNIT 23   The Passive

Do this exercise:

1   Why is the writer feeling sad?
2   How long has he had his car?
3   Why does he think it was taken?
4   Where was it found?
5   Why was it difficult to identify?
6   What else had been removed?
7   Why is it going to be difficult to get spares?
8   What does the writer say about the probable cost?
9   What kind of yard does he think he will have to start visiting?
10   What do you think happens to old cars at a breaker's yard?

G   Idea for discussion

The slave trade was one of the most shameful episodes in the long history of mankind. What do you know about it?

Where were the slaves captured? Where were they taken to? Why were they taken there? How were they treated?

Answer these questions, then talk about the slave trade.

Note how we form PASSIVES:

STATEMENTS	A lot of wine	is was will be	drunk	during the festival.
NEGATIVES	Milk	isn't wasn't won't be	drunk	during the festival.
QUESTIONS	What	is was will be	drunk	during the festival?

Special points to note

You will find the **passive** useful when you say something, and the other person doesn't really seem to understand. Look at this conversation:

"Oh, someone's stolen my handbag!"
"I'm sorry dear."
"George, did you hear me? My handbag's BEEN STOLEN."

George's reply, "*I'm sorry dear*" indicates that he hasn't realised what has happened, so the woman uses the **passive** to "wake him up".

*Look at some more typical **passive** situations:*

"Why didn't the policeman open fire?"
"He wasn't armed. Guns ARE ONLY CARRIED by English policemen in special circumstances."

"What a fabulous recording!"
"Yes, it WAS RECORDED in the States."

"Why can't we eat in the dining-room?"
"It's BEING USED as a furniture store at the moment."

"What are you going to do about all your books?"
"They'll BE PACKED UP and sent to Jersey by sea."

The Passive

It was Djazebeh's first day in her new class in the school in London.

"I want to give you all one word of warning," said her new class teacher. "You will find that most people in London are very kind and helpful towards foreigners. But there are thieves in London, just as there are in any other big city. Three weeks ago a purse belonging to one of the girls in my class was stolen on an underground train. Fortunately she only lost £20. It could have been much more. So do be careful. *Don't* leave your purse on the top of your bag, where it can easily be seen, and don't carry more money about with you than necessary!"

It so happened that Djazebeh had been to the bank that morning with her friend Anna and cashed several traveller's cheques. She had more than £100 in her handbag.

Anna leaned towards her. "You have been warned," she whispered. Djazebeh nodded.

A   Do this exercise:

1   Ask what Djazebeh's class teacher wanted to give the class.
2   Answer the question.
3   How does the teacher think most English people behave towards foreigners?
4   What happened three weeks ago?
5   Ask where this happened.
6   Answer the question.
7   Ask how much the girl lost.
8   Answer the question.
9   Where did the teacher say you shouldn't leave your purse?
10   Why not?
11   How much money should you carry about with you?
12   Where had Djazebeh and Anna been that morning?
13   Ask how much money Djazebeh had with her at that time.
14   Answer the question.
15   What did Anna whisper to Djazebeh?
16   What was Djazebeh's reaction?

UNIT 23 The Passive

B Look at these examples:

THREE WEEKS AGO A PURSE WAS STOLEN.

DON'T LEAVE YOUR PURSE WHERE IT CAN BE SEEN.

YOU HAVE BEEN WARNED.

*Now turn the following ideas into the **passive** form:*

1 Somebody has stolen my camera.
2 Turner presented a lot of his paintings to the nation.
3 You can see a picture of the Brontë sisters in the National Portrait Gallery.
4 I bought that beautiful mirror in Oxford.
5 He's sent his passport to the Immigration Office.
6 The attendants search all visitors before they go into the museum.
7 You can visit the Stock Exchange between ten and three.
8 They executed a lot of unfortunate people outside the Tower.
9 Dr Johnson often visited this pub.
10 They discovered a Roman temple when they were building that office block.

C Asking questions

*Turn the following active questions into **passive** questions (note that we do not always say by whom the action was done)*

1 When did they open the first underground railway in London?
2 Did they grow those tomatoes in England?
3 When did they execute Charles I?
4 Can you grow melons in England?
5 Where do they make china like that?
6 Why did they sack the Minister of Transport?
7 Do they make wine in England?
8 When did they build Buckingham Palace?
9 When did Stephenson invent the steam engine?
10 Have they changed the Guard yet?

D Composition

Imagine that you are visiting a stately home. You are in the blue sitting-room. The guide says:

"This room was redecorated by the fourth Duke, Rufus. The wallpaper is hand-painted, and was brought over from France. The carpet was made in Belgium, and the unusual pattern was designed by the Duke's eldest daughter, Elizabeth. She was, unfortunately, drowned in a boating accident on the lake two years later. The large portrait over the fireplace was painted by Otto Kummer in 1764."

Now think of an interesting room in your own country, real or imaginary, and write a similar speech for the guide.

The Letter

The alarm clock rang loudly close to his head. He put out his hand and turned off the alarm. For some moments he lay there, half-awake. "I must get up," he thought. Then he sat up, and lowered his feet to the floor. He took off his pyjama jacket, put on his slippers, walked over to the basin, and
5 turned on the hot tap. He drew back the curtains and looked out into the street. As he watched, the postman came up the path and delivered the post. Quickly he turned off the tap, slipped on his dressing-gown, and hurried downstairs. There was a letter from Claire. He sat down on the bottom step and opened the envelope.
10 "My dear," she began, "after our conversation last week, this letter will come as a surprise. I told you that I could look after myself, that my career must come first, that I was looking for something, I didn't know what; well, I've changed my mind. I will marry you after all . . ."
He sat there, at the bottom of the stairs, unable to grasp the full truth.
15 Suddenly the kitchen door opened, and his landlady came out into the hall. "Well, well, Mr Mitchell," she said, in her broad Irish accent, "that's a strange place to read your mail, to be sure . . . ." She broke off, as she noticed how pale he looked. "Not bad news I hope?"
He looked at her for a moment, then a huge grin spread across his face.
20 "No . . . marvellous news," he said, "I'm going to get married."

A Oral questions

1 Where was Mr Mitchell?
2 What woke him up?
3 What did he do to stop the noise?
4 What did he do with his pyjama jacket?
5 What did he do with his slippers?
6 What did he do to the hot tap?
7 What did he draw back?
8 What did he see, when he looked out of the window?
9 What did he do, just before he went downstairs?
10 What did he find?
11 What did he do with the letter?
12 Where did he sit down?
13 Why did Claire think the letter might come as a surprise?
14 Had Claire decided to marry someone else?
15 What had she decided to do?
16 Who came out of the kitchen?
17 Was she English?
18 Why did she suddenly stop speaking?
19 What did she ask him?
20 What happened to his face?

UNIT 24   Phrasal Verbs

B Note carefully the things that Mr Mitchell did after he woke up. Then describe the things that you did after you woke up this morning.

C   Look at this conversation:

Mr Collins is the sales manager, and Mr Franks his assistant.

MR COLLINS	Ah, come in, I've had a letter from head office I want you to look at.
MR FRANKS	It seems as if we really are going to have to cut down on our sales force this time.
MR COLLINS	The question is . . . can we get away with making just one of the reps[1] redundant?
MR FRANKS	I hope so, but I don't think we can put off making a decision any longer.
MR COLLINS	Do you want to put forward any suggestions?
MR FRANKS	You know my views. There's only one of our reps I'd like to get rid of.
MR COLLINS	Mr Welch?
MR FRANKS	Of course. I ran out of patience with him a long time ago.
MR COLLINS	Have you looked through his sales record recently?
MR FRANKS	Yes, his orders have been falling off steadily over the last four years, and he's not prepared to put in any extra effort at all. If I suggest it, he always tries to get out of it.
MR COLLINS	Right. I suppose I'd better break the news to him.

Do this exercise:

1   What did Mr Collins want Mr Franks to do?
2   Why might you look at a telephone book?
3   What action does Mr Franks think they will have to take, as a result of the letter from head office?
4   What might you cut down on?
5 · What is Mr Collins wondering?

[1] reps: representatives (salesmen)

140

6   A criminal is in prison. What didn't he get away with?
7   What is it that Mr Franks thinks they can't put off doing?
8   Describe the last occasion you put off doing something.
9   What does Mr Collins invite Mr Franks to put forward?
10 Put forward some suggestions for extending the social life of your class.

D   Here are some more questions about the conversation between Mr Collins and Mr Franks and ideas to think about.

1   Who does Mr Franks want to get rid of?
2   Why does he want to get rid of him?
3   If an old lady died, and you had the job of sorting things out, what might you want to get rid of?
4   What was it that Mr Franks ran out of a long time ago?
5   Think of some things that economists tell us we are going to run out of one day.
6   Has Mr Franks looked through the unfortunate Mr Welch's sales record?
7   What did he discover?
8   What sort of things might you look through?
9   What is it that Mr Welch always tries to get out of doing?
10 What sort of things might a soldier try to get out of doing?
11 What does Mr Collins decide he must do?
12 Sometimes the police have the unenviable task of breaking bad news to people. Think of some examples.

E   Below are some of the phrasal verbs used by Mr Collins and Mr Franks, and a list of "endings".

Combine each phrasal verb with one of the endings to express 10 ideas in the past.

Verbs: break it to/cut down on/look at/look through/get out of/get rid of/put forward/put in/put off/run out of

Endings: the map to try and locate our position/my appointment with the dentist/some old photos last night/a proposal of my own/my expenses last month/a lot of old rubbish this morning/typing paper last week/working on Saturday, I'm glad to say/him that his brother was dead/a lot of hard work this week.

F Idea for discussion.

Once upon a time employers were very ruthless about giving employees the sack. Now that the big unions are very strong, things are different. It's almost impossible sometimes for an employer to dismiss a worker, even though he may deserve it.

Think of a big store. Let some of the class represent the management and others the staff.

Discuss staff discipline; what is fair for a company to demand of its employees; how and when the company should have the right to give members of staff the sack.

Special points to note

This unit concentrates on phrasal verbs, but in fact students will already have met many of them.

By adding a preposition to certain verbs, we can change the meaning. It's not really a good idea for the students to sit down and try to learn fifty of these phrasal verbs in an evening. It's more sensible to start a list and add to it as you meet new and interesting examples. Here is a list of some of the most useful to start you off:

The car _broke down_, so I had to walk.
The meeting _broke up_ about six o'clock.
He was _called up_ when he was eighteen. (for military service)
They _called off_ the game, because of the weather.
They soon _cleared off_ when Tom appeared.
I must just _clear up_ in the kitchen.
He'd had a nasty blow on the head, but he soon _came round_. (recovered consciousness)
I was _cut off_ in the middle of my conversation. (on the phone)
At last the sound _died away_. (it became quiet)

Unfortunately the plan _fell through_.
I'm _fed up_ with all these delays.
I wanted to _find out_ where she lived.
He was accused of _taking part_ in the robbery two years ago, but he _got off_. (was found not guilty)
She never really _got over_ the death of her husband.
Daughters are good at _getting round_ their fathers. (making them do what they want)
They argued and argued, but eventually George _gave in_. (surrendered)
The bomb was set to _go off_ in ten minutes. (explode)
I'm sorry – I was _held up_. (delayed)

The manager decided to _leave out_ Smith and Jones. (they weren't picked for the team)
Now don't _let me down_, will you? (don't break your promise)
Could you possibly _look after_ the baby for half an hour?
What are you _looking for_? I can't find my purse.
Did you _pay back_ the money you owed John?
We're _putting on_ a dance to raise money for the fund.
He had to _put off_ the interview.
We can _put you up_. (offer you a bed for the night)
Who do you think I _ran into_ yesterday. (met by accident)

I must _see about_ the tickets. (buy them, or have them checked)
We _set off_ early. (began our journey)
Have you _settled down_ in your new flat yet? (got organised . . . do you feel comfortable there)
I was completely _taken in_. (fooled)
The interview _took place_ at the Embassy.
Who do you think _turned up_ yesterday? (sudenly appeared)
They _turned down_ his proposal. (refused it)
I'm afraid these shoes may _wear out_ very quickly – they were very cheap.
The population of the village was completely _wiped out_ in the attack. (destroyed)

UNIT 24 Phrasal Verbs

The Flood

The announcer wished everyone goodnight, and the picture faded from the screen. Mr Barley stood up, turned off the television, and looked round the room. Then he turned out the lights and went up to bed. It was raining outside. He looked out across the road towards the river.

5   "If this rain continues, there could easily be a flood," he thought.

He drew the curtains, took off his clothes, washed, put on his pyjamas and got into bed.

Some hours later he awoke. He sensed that something was wrong. It wasn't a noise that had woken him up, it was more the lack of any noise at all.

10 He got up, went over to the window, and looked down into the garden. The rain had stopped. The night was still and clear, and the moon was nearly full. But the garden wasn't there any more, and the road wasn't there; instead there was a lake, which stretched as far as the eye could see, with odd trees and bushes sticking out of it here and there. The house was completely

15 cut off.

"My goodness," he thought, "I wonder what it's like downstairs."

A Do this exercise.

1 Ask what Mr Barley was doing.
2 Answer the question.
3 Ask what he did, as soon as the programme finished.
4 Answer the question. (three things)
5 What did he do just before he went up to bed?
6 What was the thought that came into his head, as he looked out of his bedroom window?
7 What did he do before he washed?
8 What did he put on before he got into bed?
9 What three things did he do, after he woke up?
10 What did he see?
11 What were sticking up out of the water?
12 What did he think to himself when he saw the water?

B Do this exercise:

1 What do you put on, after you get up?
2 What would you do before getting into the bath?
3 What must you do, in order to fill the bath with water?
4 What might cause someone making a speech to break off suddenly?
5 What do you turn off before you go to sleep?
6 If a young man was killed in a motor accident, who might break the news to his family?
7 What might the doctor tell you to cut down on?
8 What might cause a village in Switzerland to be cut off suddenly?
9 What might a little boy tell his mother, in order to get out of going to school?
10 What would you do if you ran out of money in a foreign country?

C Answer the following questions briefly:

1 What might put you off?
2 What might you put forward?
3 What might somebody slip on, to answer the door bell, early in the morning?
4 What might a criminal hope to get away with?
5 What have you looked through recently?
6 What might a dissatisfied young employee put in for?
7 What section of a newspaper do you usually look at?
8 If a football team has been playing badly for some weeks, what might begin to fall off?
9 Who might look after a child while the mother went shopping?
10 If you moved into a furnished flat, what might you want to get rid of?

D Composition

Read the passage about Mr Barley and the flood again, then continue the story.

UNIT 25 Verbs usually followed by the Gerund:

HATE + -ING, ENJOY + -ING, ETC.

Bill the Referee

It had been a very hard football match. One player from each side had been given a red card, and two others got yellow cards. After the game, the referee, Bill Cross, was interviewed on television by Frank Duff.

F D   This has been a fairly typical Saturday afternoon for you, hasn't it? Do
5   you really enjoy refereeing?

B C   Yes, I find I still look forward to it.

F D   I can't help feeling that you'd enjoy the game much more, sitting in the stand.

B C   Well, of course, every game produces different problems for the
10   referee.

F D   Now, you didn't give Smith a red card for the foul, did you? You gave him the red card for arguing?

Verbs usually followed by the Gerund: UNIT 25

HATE + -ING, ENJOY + -ING, ETC.

    B C   Yes, I don't like people arguing with the referee. I had warned him, but he went on arguing, so off he went.

15   F D   Then there was the incident with Brown. Why didn't you allow the trainer onto the field?

    B C   I hate seeing a player pretending to be hurt, in order to get a free kick. A couple of minutes later, when the ball came near him, he was quite all right again.

20   F D   Then when you refused to give a penalty in the second half, the crowd got very angry with you. Doesn't that worry you?

    B C   No, if the football match is exciting the crowd are going to get excited, naturally. I don't mind the crowd shouting at me at all. As a referee, you expect it.

A Oral questions

1 What does Bill referee?
2 What sort of game had this one been?
3 Why did each team finish the game with ten men?
4 What did Frank Duff do?
5 Ask if Bill enjoys refereeing.
6 Answer the question.
7 Ask if he still looks forward to it.
8 Answer the question.
9 Why was Smith sent off?
10 What had Bill done earlier, concerning Smith?
11 Explain what happened in the incident concerning Brown.
12 Why did the crowd become very angry with Bill in the second half?
13 What is the effect likely to be on the crowd, if the game is exciting?
14 What does Bill think that a referee must expect?

UNIT 25   Verbs usually followed by the Gerund:

HATE + -ING, ENJOY + -ING, ETC.

B   Look at these conversations

BILL   I enjoy refereeing
TOM   So do I.
BILL   I enjoy refereeing.
REG   *Do* you?

Note:

By stressing the 'do', Reg is not only asking a question but indicating that he is surprised that *anyone* could enjoy it.

Make similar conversations, replacing refereeing with the items below:

playing football
cooking
watching television
fishing
listening to music
going to the opera
driving
going to parties

C   Bill says that he looks forward to refereeing. We might say:

"I'm looking forward to the concert this evening" or "I'm looking forward to going to the concert this evening".

We look forward to things we know we are going to enjoy. Think of some things you are looking forward to doing and make up sentences about them, following the model.

D   Look at these conversations

BILL   I don't like people arguing.
TOM   Neither do I.
BILL   I hate seeing a player pretending to be hurt when he isn't.
TOM   So do I.

I HATE and I DON'T LIKE both express a similar idea, but I HATE is stronger.

Note:

In the two examples above Tom agrees with Bill. If he wanted to disagree he could say: "Oh, it doesn't worry me."

Use the ideas below to make similar conversations. As far as possible express ideas which are true.

driving in heavy rain
waiting in long queues
making calls from public telephone boxes
listening to people complaining
writing "thank you" letters
travelling in the rush-hour
visiting hospitals
going to the dentist
etc.

E   Bill says: "I don't mind the crowd shouting . . ."

He means that it doesn't worry him. However we often use the expression "I don't mind . . . -ing" when offering to do something for somebody.

Look at this conversation:

BILL   Who is going to pay the bill?
TOM   I don't mind paying it.

Make similar conversations:

1   . . . give me a lift?
2   . . . lend me £5 till Monday?
3   . . . tell George the bad news?
4   . . . pay for the coffee?
5   . . . get the tickets?
6   . . . clean the car?
7   . . . ring the restaurant and book a table?
8   . . . open the wine?

F   Note how ideas like this can be expressed in the *past*:

Did you enjoy refereeing the game today?
I didn't mind the crowd shouting . . .
I hated asking for the day off.
I haven't been looking forward to seeing him again.

*Below are some statements and questions in indirect speech (reported speech). They are all about Julia. Turn them into **direct** speech.*

1   She said she'd enjoyed flying in Concorde.
2   She said she hadn't minded making the tea.
3   She told me she had hated appearing in that play.
4   She said she'd been looking forward to meeting you.
5   She said she hadn't liked going home alone.

HATE + -ING, ENJOY + -ING, ETC.

6   She said she hadn't minded looking after Fred at all.
7   She asked if we'd enjoyed staying at the Hotel Adler.
8   She said she hadn't been looking forward to taking the exam.
9   She asked if I'd minded cleaning the car.
10 She told me she'd enjoyed painting the pictures.
11 She asked if we'd been looking forward to going to Finland.
12 She asked if we'd minded missing the football on TV.

G   Study this conversation

"Do you worry about things like that?"
"No, I stopped worrying about things like that a long time ago."

Use the ideas below to make similar conversations.

1   . . . go to the pub any more?
2   . . . smoke?
3   . . . still work at Barret's?
4   . . . play football now?
5   . . . still ride a bicycle?
6   . . . buy your groceries at Tesco's?
7   . . . often go dancing these days?
8   . . . still go out with Catherine?
9   . . . often go riding?
10 . . . still go to the greyhound racing?

H   Ideas for discussion

What sort of things do you like doing?
What sort of things do you dislike doing?
What sort of things do you enjoy doing?
What do you hate doing?
Talk about these things. Is there anything you're specially looking forward to?

Special points to note

There are a number of common verbs that are usually followed by the gerund. Here is a list of some of the most useful:

I'm looking forward to seeing you.
She likes dancing.
She doesn't like going out in the evening.
I believe *he really enjoys* cleaning his car.
I hate getting up on cold winter mornings.
Would you mind posting a letter for me?
I can't help feeling cross about it.

She can't stand working there any longer.
I've finished using the bathroom.
They prevented me from going into my own office.
I avoided mentioning the subject as long as I could.
He risked getting into trouble for your sake.
John admitted making the telephone call.
He denied writing the letter.

Forgive my asking you, but where did you get that bag?
Hilda *suggested* going to the pictures.
He kept annoying me, so I hit him.
I understand his not wanting to come.
Did you ever *consider* selling it?
I really *missed* seeing her.
It's no use complaining about it now.
I've stopped taking those sleeping pills.

but notice:

We walked for an hour or so, then we *stopped to take* some photographs,

which means:

We stopped *in order to . . .*

UNIT 25   Verbs usually followed by the Gerund:

HATE + -ING, ENJOY + -ING, ETC.

An interview with an actor

Gordon Bishop is an actor, and he took part in Vernon Miller's late night TV chat show recently. Here is an extract from their discussion:

	MILLER	Welcome to the show, Gordon.
	BISHOP	Thank you . . . it's nice to be here.
5	MILLER	Now, you've been an actor for quite a few years . . .
	BISHOP	Thirty-two . . .
	MILLER	Thirty-two years. That seems incredible . . . well, what sort of parts do you like playing best?
	BISHOP	Oh, baddies, I think.
10	MILLER	You don't enjoy being the hero?
	BISHOP	Well, I don't mind being the hero . . . but I think I prefer being wicked . . . it's more interesting.
	MILLER	You've been in films, you've been on the stage, you've had several parts on television. There's even an advertisement . . .
15	BISHOP	Yes, don't let's talk about that . . . I've stopped doing advertisements. I hate seeing that . . .
	MILLER	. . . the crazy milkman . . .
	BISHOP	Yes, I only did it because I was between shows. I'd finished making a film, and I was in a new play, which unfortunately
20		closed after only two weeks.
	MILLER	Do you like working on the stage?
	BISHOP	Oh, yes. If I have a good part in a successful play, I really look forward to going to work. There's nothing like a live audience. They give you so much.
25	MILLER	And television?
	BISHOP	Yes, television can be fun. But, as you know, there's not too much live television . . .
	MILLER	We're live . . .
	BISHOP	Yes, we're live, but . . . plays and things . . . Making a play
30		for television is very like making a film. If you mess up your lines, they'll shoot the scene again. On the stage, if you forget your lines, you're on your own . . .
	MILLER	And what about long runs? Have you ever had a really long run in the theatre?
35	BISHOP	Yes, I spent three years at the Criterion Theatre in Agatha Christie's *Murder at Midnight*.
	MILLER	I can't help thinking it must be a bit boring to go on, night after night, playing the same part . . .
	BISHOP	Yes, but I didn't mind doing the Agatha Christie . . . there was
40		a marvellous atmosphere . . . we had a wonderful cast . . . sometimes you're lucky . . .

Verbs usually followed by the Gerund: UNIT 25

HATE + -ING, ENJOY + -ING, ETC.

A Do this exercise:

1 Ask how long Gordon Bishop has been an actor.
2 Answer the question.
3 What sort of characters does he enjoy playing?
4 Why?
5 What type of work has he decided not to do in the future?
6 What character did he play in the one he hates?
7 What happened to the new play he was in?
8 Why do you think this happened?
9 What is it that he specially likes about working in the theatre?
10 What happens in the television studio, if you mess up your lines?
11 What is it that Vernon Miller suggests must be a bit boring?
12 Why did Gordon Bishop enjoy working in *Murder at Midnight*?

B Taking your facts from the discussion, complete these sentences:

1 Gordon enjoys . . .
2 He hates . . .
3 He doesn't mind . . .
4 He likes . . .
5 He looks forward to . . . when . . .
6 He's stopped . . .

C Now write about yourself. Try and use real facts about your life.

1 Mention one thing you enjoy doing.
2 Mention two things you hate doing.

3 Mention one thing you are looking forward to doing.
4 Mention one thing you don't mind doing.
5 What might make you decide to stop going to a certain shop?
6 What do you like drinking in hot weather?

D Composition

Write an extract from a similar chat show discussion between Vernon Miller and a famous sportsman. (You can decide on the sport, but mention it in your introduction.)

UNIT 26 Second Conditional:

IF I WERE YOU, I'D . . .

A plan for London traffic

London, like so many big cities, has traffic problems that seem to get worse every year. Tom Jenkins, a London bus driver, was asked what he would do to improve the situation, if he were put in charge of London Transport. This is what he said:

5　　"If you put me in charge of London Transport, I'd make a number of changes. I'd ban private cars from central London between 7.00 am and 6.30 pm unless the owner actually lived in the area. I'd build a lot of new, cheap, car parks near the railway stations on the outskirts of London, so that people could leave their cars there and travel to and from work by train. I'd

10　　fix a standard fare for all bus or tube¹ journeys in the centre, and I'd make it possible for people to buy ten or a dozen tickets at one time at a reduced rate. Then the buses and taxis would be able to move much more quickly and easily, and life would become more comfortable for everyone."

A Oral questions

1　What do all big cities seem to have?
2　What is Tom's job?
3　What would he do about private cars?
4　Where would he build the new car parks?
5　Why would he build them there?
6　What would he do about fares?
7　What other innovation would he introduce regarding tickets?
8　What effect would these changes have?

¹ tube: London's underground electric railway

UNIT 26 Second Conditional:

IF I WERE YOU, I'D . . .

B Look at this pattern:

If you put me in charge, I'd make a number of changes.

This is a statement that might be made in many situations. Imagine a hotel which badly needs reorganising. Suggest ways in which improvements could be made. You say:

If you put me in charge, I'd . . .

1   The prices are too high.
2   There is plenty of space, but no tennis court.
3   The cooking is awful.
4   The heating system is quite inadequate.
5   The carpets are old and worn.
6   There is no swimming pool.
7   The staff are very rude and unhelpful.
8   There is no 'games' room.
9   There are no showers in the rooms.
10 The lighting in the bar is very harsh* and bright.

C Imagine you have a teenage friend who is seriously considering leaving home. You don't think he/she has really considered the consequences of this action.

Make a conversation asking and answering questions like this:

Where would you go?
How would you find somewhere to live?
How would you earn a living?
What sort of job could you get?
How would your parents feel about it?

and any others you can think of.

D Excuses, excuses.

Look carefully at these ideas:

Sally wants Frank to come to the party. Frank has too much work to do. He says:

"I'd come if I didn't have so much work to do" or "I'd come if I were free".

Sally thinks Frank should telephone his sister, but he hasn't got her new telephone number. He says: "I'd telephone her if I had her new number."

Make similar sentences.

1   Sally thinks Frank should write to congratulate two friends on their engagement. But he doesn't have their address. He says:
2   Sally would like Frank to go to the pictures, but Frank doesn't think there's anything good on. He says:
3   Frank wants Sally to come with him to the football match, but she feels that it's too cold to go out. She says:
4   Sally wants Frank to come to dinner with a French couple who speak almost no English. Sally's French is very good, Frank's is awful. He says:
5   Frank has been invited to play in a football match. Sally thinks he should play, but Frank knows he is very unfit. He says:
6   Frank fancies a nice curry for supper, but Sally hasn't got any curry powder. She says:
7   Frank wants Sally to come to the annual office party, but Sybil Plum will be going, and Sally hates Sybil. She says:
8   Frank has been asked to work overtime. But he has refused, because he would have to pay so much in income tax that it wouldn't be worth doing. He says:
9   Frank has seen a secondhand car he would very much like to buy, but it is so expensive that he can't afford it. He says:
10 Frank and Sally are going to the seaside for the day. Sally wants Frank to take his camera along, but it isn't working properly. Frank says:

E Idea for discussion

Buddhists believe in reincarnation. In other words, when you die, you come back to another life.

Imagine that you were going to be reincarnated, and could choose what sort of person you were going to be, where you were going to live, and what job you were going to have.

What would you choose?

---

* harsh: hard and unfriendly.

Second Conditional:

IF I WERE YOU, I'D . . .

Note how we form SECOND CONDITIONAL sentences

| STATEMENTS | If | I | had | a headache, | I'd (I would)* | take | an aspirin |

| NEGATIVES | If | you | didn't | come, | we'd (would)* be | very disappointed. |

| QUESTIONS | Would | you | speak | to him about it, | if | you | were | me? |

★ Note: In the first person, SHOULD and SHOULDN'T may be used instead of WOULD and WOULDN'T.

"If I had a headache, I SHOULD take an aspirin."

Special points to note

You will use the second conditional when you are giving advice:

IF I WERE YOU, I'D ASK AT THE FARM.

You will also use it when you want to talk about things that might or might not happen, depending on something else.

Compare these sentences:

If John brings his records, we'll have enough music . . . (But I'm not sure he's going to bring them)

If John brought his records, we'd have enough music . . . (But I know he doesn't like bringing his records to parties)

In the first case, the speaker believes that John will probably bring his records. In the second case he thinks John might bring them, but probably won't.

In the next unit we are going to concentrate on **conditional** questions.

IF I WERE YOU, I'D . . .

Thomas More

The early part of the sixteenth century was an exciting time in England.
Henry VIII was king and if the King liked you, you could rise to an
important position very rapidly; but if you did something to annoy Henry,
you could lose your head equally quickly. Thomas More lived at this time.

5   The King quarrelled with the Pope. He wanted the Pope to declare that
his marriage to Catherine was not legal, because Catherine was previously
married to his brother. If the Pope did this, he would be free to marry Ann
Boleyn; but the Pope wouldn't agree. So the King announced that in future
he was going to be the head of the Church of England.

10   Most of the politicians and church leaders of the time supported the
King. But Thomas More was too honest to do this. He refused to sign the
document stating that Henry was to be head of the Church. Eventually he
was arrested and taken to the Tower. There he was executed.

       His head was placed on a spike on London Bridge with those of other
15 "traitors". However his daughter persuaded one of the guards to throw her
father's head down to her, while she waited in a boat below. She took the
head home to Canterbury, and it was buried under the floor of St Dunstan's
church.

A   Answer these questions

1   Why might it have been dangerous to be at the English Court, at the
    beginning of the sixteenth century?
2   Why might it have been exciting?
3   What happened between Henry and the Pope?
4   What did Henry want the Pope to do?
5   Why did Henry want the Pope to do this?
6   What did the King declare?
7   Why didn't Thomas More support this move?
8   Where was he taken?
9   What did he refuse to do?
10 So what happened to him?
11 Where was his head put?
12 What finally happened to his head?

B   Note this pattern carefully:

If the Pope DID this, he WOULD BE free to marry Ann Boleyn.

*Complete the ideas below to make more **conditional** sentences:*

1   If my car was going all right, . . . lift.
2   If I had the money, . . . lend it to you.
3   If she spent a few months in France, she . . .
4   If he were really hungry, . . .
5   If I took the exam again tomorrow,
    . . . probably . . .
6   If I had a television, we . . .
7   If my watch was going, I . . .
8   If they got married, I think . . .

C   Read this text

Nobody ever visits Bedford, because we don't have a great cathedral, or a wonderful castle, and Shakespeare wasn't born there; but it's still my favourite town.

If you came to see me there, it would be best to come in the summer time. We could hire a punt, like the ones they have in Cambridge, and go for a picnic up the river. And in the evening you could come with me to spend a couple of lazy hours in Bedford Park, watching a cricket match.

The next day I'd take you to the Cecil Higgins Museum, where you would see a wonderful collec-tion of old English watercolours, and some mar-vellous examples of early Meissen porcelain.

In the afternoon we'd go out into the country, to visit some of the little villages nearby; and we'd stop for tea at a little tea-room I know, run by two elderly ladies, where you can have delicious, toasted scones with strawberry jam, and home-made chocolate cake.

Do this exercise:

1   Why does nobody visit Bedford?
2   Ask when it would be best to go there.
3   Answer the question.
4   Ask what you could do at that time of the year.
5   Answer the question. (two things)
6   Ask what you could see at the museum.
7   Answer the question. (two things)
8   Ask where we could go in the afternoon.
9   Answer the question. (one thing)
10   Ask where we would stop for tea.
11   Answer the question.
12   Ask what we would have for tea.
13   Answer the question.

D   Composition

Read the passage about the writer's home town once more, then write a piece about your home town, or some place you like, telling a friend what you would show him/her if he/she came to visit you there.

Mr Pollard and the Solicitor

People think that all solicitors are rich and prosperous. In any town there are, of course, rich and prosperous solicitors, but there are also solicitors like me. I am neither rich nor prosperous. I have an office over a fish and chip shop, for which I pay an exorbitant rent, and two rather inefficient
5 secretaries.

I suppose it is because my premises are in the less fashionable part of the town, but my clients always seem to have enormous problems and miserable incomes. Mr Pollard was exactly that sort of client. He was a small, untidy little man, with a large head and round, old-fashioned spectacles.
10   "I have a problem," he began nervously, "I bought this house, you see. I got a mortgage from the building society, but then I lost my job, so I got behind with the payments." He gave me the details. It appeared that he owed eleven payments of £50, and had no job and no money. Not surprisingly the building society had written to say they intended to take
15 possession of the house, sell it, and thus get back their money.

"What would happen if they sold it for less than I paid?" he asked. "Would I get back any money?"

"Probably not," I replied.

"Would you mind telephoning the building society?" he pleaded, "and
20 see if they could possibly give me a little more time?"

"If you're not earning any money, how will more time help?" I asked. He looked at me hopelessly.

In the end the house was sold. The building society debt was paid off, and Mr Pollard got £60.

A   Oral questions

1 What is the man in the street's opinion of solicitors?
2 What about the writer?
3 Why does he usually get very poor clients?
4 What was Mr Pollard like?
5 Who did he borrow the mortgage from?
6 How much did he owe?
7 What were the building society threatening to do?
8 What did Mr Pollard want to know?
9 What did he ask the writer to do?
10 Did the solicitor think this was a good idea?
11 What happened to the house in the end?
12 How much did Mr Pollard get?

B Look at this idea:

"If you're not earning any money, how will more time help?"

Here the solicitor is objecting to Mr Pollard's suggestion. Now pretend to be the solicitor and object to the following suggestions made by clients earning no money.

Example:

"I'M THINKING OF GETTING A NEW CAR."

"IF YOU'RE NOT EARNING ANY MONEY, HOW ARE YOU GOING TO AFFORD A NEW CAR?"

1 I plan to pay off the debt in the next few weeks.
2 I've promised to lend my brother £100.
3 I intend to install central heating in my house.
4 I want to rent a colour TV.
5 I'd like to give Elsie and the family a decent holiday at the seaside.
6 I looked at a new flat this morning. The rent's £90 a month, but it's very nice.
7 I mean to start a business of my own.
8 I'm going to Paris soon, then I'll sort it out.
9 I'm going to see my bank manager to try and raise a loan.
10 I need to get away for a while – I'm thinking of going on a cruise.

C Look at this question:

"What would happen, if they sold it for less than I paid?"

A number of clients put similar questions to the solicitor. What did they ask in each case?

1 Mrs Jones's husband left her. She is seeking a divorce. But her husband might decide to come back.
2 Mrs Jones has the children with her. She is worried in case her husband tries to take the children away from her.
3 Mr Cordell was involved in a motor accident. He has two witnesses, but they might not turn up at the court.

4 It seems possible that the other motorist wasn't insured. Mr Cordell wants to know how this would affect him.
5 Mrs Craggs had a diamond ring stolen. The insurance company have paid £300 compensation. The police might catch the thief and get the ring back.
6 Mrs Wilson has just been informed that, as she appears to be the only surviving relative of a wealthy business man who died recently, she is going to inherit a lot of money. But other relatives might come forward.
7 Mr Johnson has signed a contract to sell his house, but the buyer might change his mind.
8 Mr Clark recently bought a new car which has given him a lot of trouble. He is worried in case the firm he bought it from might refuse to accept any further responsibility.
9 Mr Thompson's next-door neighbour is complaining about a new garage he is building. He might take Mr Thompson to court.
10 Mr Jackson has been cheated by a business partner. He is taking this man to court, but he is afraid that his former partner might leave the country before the case is heard.

D Idea for discussion

You work for a television company, and you are called to a conference to discuss whether or not a certain programme is feasible. The idea is that a young man should be taken to a small island off the Scottish coast. He would remain there for a time, living entirely off the land.

Television cameras would record what happened to him, and he would talk about his feelings each day.

The teacher represents the producer who thought up the idea. Ask questions like this:

"How long would he stay there?"
"What would he take with him?"
"How would . . ."
"Where would . . . ?"

Remember that your objective would be to create a piece of TV reporting that would provide compelling viewing.

UNIT 27   First and Second Conditional questions

Note the forms of some typical FIRST and SECOND CONDITIONAL questions.

Who* will you go to What will you do How will you manage	if you run out of money?

Who would you go to What would you do How would you manage	if you ran out of money?

Shall is normally used for the first person in **First Conditional** questions:

What shall $\frac{I}{we}$ do,	if $\frac{I}{we}$ run out of money?

Special points to note

You will need to be able to ask First and Second Conditional questions when you want to find out what may or may not happen on future occasions.

Compare these two ideas:

"What WILL you do if you RUN out of money?"

"What WOULD you do if you RAN out of money?"

In the first case (First Conditional), the speaker thinks you will probably run out of money.

In the second case (Second Conditional), the speaker thinks you may possibly run out of money.

Note also the useful idea:

"Would you mind lending me £5 till Monday?"

This isn't actually a conditional question, but it is a very useful and polite way of asking somebody to do something for you.

WRITTEN SECTION

David Renton

David Renton was forty-nine years old. He had worked at the bank for thirty years, and as he stood behind the counter, serving a queue of impatient customers, he thought to himself, "Surely there must be a better way of spending one's time than this."

5   Outside it was a beautiful spring day. The sky was blue, the birds were singing, the trees were in bud.

That evening David surprised his wife by bringing her a big bunch of daffodils.

"My goodness," she said, "what are these for?"

10   "How would you like to live in the country?" he asked.

"In the country?"

"How would you feel if I gave up my job?"

"But your pension . . . you'd lose your pension."

"No, there's an early retirement scheme – I could draw a reduced

15   pension," he said.

"But we couldn't live on that. You'd have to get another job. What could you do?"

"A smallholding," he said, "I'd get a smallholding and grow vegetables."

A Do this exercise:

1 What was David doing, when the idea came into his head?
2 What state were the trees in?
3 How did David surprise his wife?
4 Why do you think he did this?
5 What was his wife's immediate reaction to his suggestion that he should give
   up his job?
6 How did he reply to this objection?
7 What did she suggest that he would have to do?
8 What does he intend to do?

UNIT 27 First and Second Conditional questions

B David Renton put this question to his wife:

"How would you feel, if I gave up my job at the bank?"

He could have asked other, similar, questions. What were they? The notes will help you.

1 How/you/feel/leave/bank
2 What/you/say/change/job
3 How/you/feel/buy/smallholding
4 How/the children/feel/we/go/to live/country

Similarly his wife might have said to him:

5 How/we/live/give up/your job
6 How/you/find/job/we/leave/city
7 Where/we/live/sell/house
8 What/children/do/we/go/away

C David and his wife were discussing his plan to buy a smallholding. What were the questions she asked? His replies will help you.

1 What . . . ?
   I'd concentrate on lettuces, cauliflowers and beans.

2 How . . . keep . . . away?
   I'd put big nets over the little plants.

3 . . . keep . . . animals?
   Pigs, probably.

4 . . . fruit?
   Yes, soft fruits like strawberries, raspberries and gooseberries.

5 How . . . produce[1] to market?
   I'd get myself a small van.

6 . . . the bank lend . . . ?
   Yes, I'm sure I could borrow a little money from the bank, if I wanted to.

7 . . . have to work . . . ?
   Yes, I would at first, but later I could get some help.

8 Where . . . buy the smallholding?
   Near some nice little village, in the country.

D Composition

Assuming that David sold his house in the city, gave up his job at the bank and moved into a little cottage some twelve miles out into the country, how would the move change his wife's life?

[1] produce: the fruit, vegetables etc. which he grows

My Grandfather's Watch

My grandfather used to have a beautiful gold pocket watch. He wore it on a fine gold chain across the front of his waistcoat, and when I was small he promised to leave it to me in his will.

"When I'm gone," he said, "this is going to be yours."

5   Unfortunately that will never happen now. About three months ago, my grandfather came up to London to visit us. The first Sunday morning after he arrived, my youngest son said he wanted to go to the park.

"We'll do better than that," said my grandfather, "we'll go and feed the pigeons in Trafalgar Square." So off they went. They got home about 10   tea-time and my grandfather was looking very upset.

"My watch," he said, "it's gone. Someone must have stolen it while we were feeding the pigeons."

"Did you tell the police?" I asked.

"No," he said, "I didn't think it would do any good."

15   "You should have reported it," I said. "Perhaps you just lost it."

"No," he replied, shaking his head. "Someone must have taken it. But I know what I'm going to do."

My grandfather put an advertisement in the Personal column of the *Evening Standard* and the *Evening News* for a week.

> If the gentleman who stole my gold pocket watch near the statue of Nelson will meet me on Sunday 6th May, in the same place at 1.00 o'clock, I will buy my watch back for the sum of £100. This theft has not been reported to the police, and no questions will be asked.

20   At a few minutes after one on the afternoon in question a small, nervous man, wearing a cloth cap, approached my grandfather. "Excuse me, Sir," he asked, "are you the gentleman enquiring about his pocket watch?"

My grandfather nodded. "Well, you must understand, Sir, that I didn't have it, but the gentleman who did has asked me to give it back."

25   From the pocket of his rather dirty overcoat, he produced my grandfather's watch. My grandfather was delighted. He paid the man £100, as promised, and fixed the watch and chain back where they belonged. Solemnly he shook hands with the little man.

"If I were you, Sir," said the little man, "I should keep your overcoat 30 buttoned up when you're in a crowd like this." Then he disappeared.

My grandfather strolled back to the bus stop. He thought he would like to have another look at his watch. So, smiling to himself, he unbuttoned his coat and looked down. The smile froze on his lips. The watch and chain were no longer there.

A   Oral questions

1   What did the writer's grandfather have?
2   Where did he wear it?
3   Why did the writer take a special interest in it?
4   Who wanted to go to the park?
5   Ask what the writer's grandfather suggested instead.
6   Answer the question.
7   Did the old man report the theft to the police?
8   What did he do?
9   Who approached the old man in Trafalgar Square?
10   Did this man admit that he was the thief?
11   What was his explanation for being there?
12   Did the little man hand over the watch?
13   What did the writer's grandfather give the little man?
14   What did the little man advise the writer's grandfather to do in the future?
15   What did the old man discover when he got back to the bus stop?

B It is very easy to be wise after the event. Your friend takes a certain action. Things don't turn out successfully. So we tell him/her what he/she should have done or shouldn't have done.

Look at these examples:

"You should have reported it to the police."
"You shouldn't have given him all that money."

Make at least one should have and one shouldn't have sentence for each of the situations below.

1 Your friend is complaining about the price she paid for her coffee at the corner shop. It's cheaper at the supermarket.
2 Your friend bought a secondhand car recently. It has been giving a lot of trouble.
3 Your friend had to go to Sheffield. He went by coach, and the journey was very slow. Trains go to Sheffield.
4 Your friend has had a problem that has been worrying him/her for days. At last he/she has told you about it.
5 Your friend came to England four months ago, knowing no English at all. The first weeks were very hard for him/her.
6 Your friend had an extra ticket for the jazz concert. It cost £4.00. He gave it away. Other people were selling spare tickets outside the theatre.
7 You are out with a friend. He isn't wearing a coat, and it's very cold.
8 A record came out called *The Beatles' Greatest Hits*. It consisted of reissues of original tracks by the Beatles. Another record was issued called *The All Stars play the Beatles' Greatest Hits*. These were pale imitations of the originals. That's the record your friend bought.

C *Someone stole my watch* is a definite statement.

But often we want to say what *probably* happened. Then we can use this construction:

"Someone MUST HAVE STOLEN my watch."

Use the situations below to make more sentences like this.

Note: Some of the situations might lead to more than one idea.

1 You left your bicycle outside the school. When you came back it wasn't there.
2 You had some guests staying in your home. After they had gone, the phone bill came in. It was much bigger than usual.
3 Your friend Kitty was coming to supper. You went to meet the bus she planned to come on, but she wasn't on it.
4 You are very busy in the office. One moment you have an important letter in your hand, the next you don't. You know it's not lost.
5 You examine a watch made by the West African Watch Company. The design is almost identical to that of a Swiss watch.
6 A burglar came into your house and stole several items. In the morning you find a window wide open at the back.
7 You are visiting Wells, in Somerset, and you are shown a model of the cathedral, made entirely out of matchsticks.
8 A prisoner under interrogation fell from the top floor window of the police headquarters to his death. You are sure he didn't jump.

D If we want to express the idea of what *possibly* happened, we can say:

"Someone MIGHT HAVE STOLEN your watch."

Look at the situation in exercise **C**, and see which you could use to make MIGHT HAVE statements.

E You are a detective. When a nasty murder has been committed, they send for you.

For example, a body is found at the bottom of the cliffs near Dover. You say:

"He MUST HAVE BEEN STANDING near the edge."

Make similar remarks for the following situations:

1 A secretary is found murdered in her office. There was a half-finished letter in the typewriter . . .
2 A well-known stamp collector has been murdered. In front of him is a stamp catalogue and a pair of tweezers, but the stamps have gone . . .
3 A jeweller is found dead. It is a few minutes to six. One of the shutters is already in position covering the shop window. The other is on the floor beside him . . .

4   A blackmailer has been murdered by one of the people he was blackmailing. He is lying on the floor beside the telephone, and the receiver is beside him . . .

5   The wife of a gangster involved in a protection racket has been killed. A bomb was thrown into her kitchen. Her husband was waiting for his dinner in the sitting-room . . .

6   A bank manager has been shot at his home and the keys to the bank stolen. He is lying on the bathroom floor. His head is covered in shampoo . . .

7   An old burglar is shot. On the floor beside him is his scrapbook. In this are newspaper cuttings, referring to his crimes . . .

8   A politician has been killed in his sitting-room. The television was still on when the police arrived . . .

F   Ideas for discussion:

Have you ever had anything stolen?
Has your house ever been broken into?
What did the thieves steal?
Do you know anybody who has suffered in this way?

When you have remembered some real robberies you will be able to say:

what must have happened or
what might have happened and
what someone should or shouldn't have done to prevent the robbery.

Note the forms of MUST HAVE/SHOULD HAVE/MIGHT HAVE

STATEMENTS	Tom	must have might have	lost his way. (That's why he hasn't arrived)
	George	should have	told me about the problem. (Then I could have found a solution)

NEGATIVES	Tom	can't have might not have	got on the right bus. (That's why he hasn't arrived)
	George	shouldn't have	said what he did to his boss. (Then he wouldn't have got the sack)

QUESTIONS	Should I	have got on	the number 12 Bus? (The bus I got on obviously wasn't the right one)

Must have . . ./Should have . . . UNIT 28

Special points to note

If you want to explain what PROBABLY happened in any situation, you can use MUST HAVE . . . .

"Oh, look. There's a dead fox."
"Poor thing. IT MUST HAVE BEEN RUN OVER."

When we want to oppose the idea that SOMETHING MUST HAVE HAPPENED, we can use CAN'T HAVE HAPPENED.

"George MUST HAVE FORGOTTEN about the party."
"No, I'm sure he CAN'T HAVE FORGOTTEN, he must have been delayed."

Note also this conversation:

"Where CAN HE HAVE GOT TO?"
"He MUST HAVE MISSED the train."

SHOULD HAVE DONE means OUGHT TO HAVE DONE

It is useful when we want to discuss why things went wrong.

"He'd had too much to drink. He SHOULDN'T HAVE DRIVEN home. He SHOULD HAVE called a taxi."

"You SHOULD HAVE seen a doctor as soon as you noticed that your ankle was swollen."[2]

---

[2] swollen: bigger than usual.

UNIT 28   Must have . . ./Should have . . .

Churchill's Portrait

Winston Churchill was one of the great men of his era, and to mark their respect for him, Parliament commissioned a fine artist, Graham Sutherland, to paint his portrait. When it was completed, it was presented to him, at a grand ceremony in the Westminster Hall, at the House of Commons.

5   There is a famous piece of news film, which shows Churchill accepting the gift. He describes the painting as "a remarkable example of modern art", which raises a loud laugh.

In fact he must have disliked the portrait intensely. Sutherland afterwards reported that he asked Churchill whether it was to be painted in 10   "happy" or "bulldog" mood. "Bulldog," replied Churchill. At the time, Churchill was coming to the end of his political career and was, apparently, displeased that people wanted him to retire.

Some twenty years later it was disclosed that Lady Churchill hated the portrait so much that she had it destroyed. "It was preying on his mind,"[1] 15   she is reported as saying.

A leading art critic was asked what he thought about the affair. "I can sympathise with Lady Churchill," he said. "Graham Sutherland is a very honest artist, who could only paint what he saw. At the time the portrait was painted, Churchill was an old man, worried by the thought of his impending 20   retirement. But Lady Churchill should never have allowed the portrait to be destroyed. If it was so distasteful to Churchill and to her, it could have been stored away until after their deaths. To destroy a work of art in this fashion seems to me a dreadful act of vandalism."

A   Answer these questions:

1   What did Parliament do as a mark of respect for Churchill?
2   Where did the grand ceremony take place?
3   Why do we know exactly what Churchill said, when he received the portrait?
4   How did he describe the painting?
5   How does the writer believe Churchill felt about the portrait?
6   What was Churchill worried about at that time?
7   What did Lady Churchill do?
8   What was the reason she gave?
9   What did the famous art critic say about her action?
10   What does he suggest she could have done instead?

[1] preying on his mind: worrying him

B Study this idea:

It was wrong of Lady Churchill to allow the portrait to be destroyed.

LADY CHURCHILL SHOULD NEVER HAVE ALLOWED the portrait to be destroyed.

Use the ideas below to make similar sentences:

1 It was wrong of the police to arrest Smith.
2 It was wrong of Colin to leave his wife.
3 It was wrong of George to take that job.
4 It was wrong of Frank to say that to James.
5 It was wrong of David to borrow Tony's records without asking him.
6 It was wrong of Keith to shout at Valerie as he did.
7 It was wrong of Cathy to take all those tablets.
8 It was wrong of Anne to marry Tom.

C Look at this idea:

He MUST HAVE disliked the portrait intensely.

Make more sentences like this, using MUST HAVE.

1 At Chartwell, which was Churchill's home, there is a fishpond. When he was an old man, he spent a lot of time sitting at this spot. (*like*)
2 At Chartwell you can see some of the pictures painted by Churchill. He painted a lot of pictures. (*enjoy*)
3 At Chartwell, too, you can see the wall Churchill built with his own hands. It's quite a big wall. (*work/hard*)
4 You can also see some of the trophies won by his racehorses. (*get/a lot of pleasure*)
5 Churchill was very lucky in his marriage, and he spent as much time as he possibly could with his wife. (*love*)
6 Churchill wrote many books. Some of them are very long. (*spend/time*)

D Composition

Write a short account of the life of a famous statesman.

Third Conditional:

IF I HADN'T OVERSLEPT, I'D HAVE BEEN ON THAT PLANE

The Man who missed the Plane

James wrote a play for television, about an immigrant family who came to England from Pakistan, and the problems they had settling down in England. The play was surprisingly successful, and it was bought by an American TV company.

5   James was invited to go to New York to help with the production. He lived in Dulwich, which is an hour's journey away from Heathrow. The flight was due to leave at 8.30 am, so he had to be at the airport about 7.30 in the morning. He ordered a mini-cab for 6.30, set his alarm for 5.45, and went to sleep. Unfortunately he forgot to wind the clock, and it stopped

10   shortly after midnight. Also the driver of the mini-cab had to work very late that night and overslept.

James woke with that awful feeling that something was wrong. He looked at his alarm clock. It stood there silently, with the hands pointing to ten past twelve. He turned on the radio and discovered that it was, in fact, ten to

15   nine. He swore quietly and switched on the electric kettle.

He was just pouring the boiling water into the teapot when the nine o'clock pips sounded on the radio. The announcer began to read the news . . . "reports are coming in of a crash near Heathrow Airport. A Boeing 707 bound for New York crashed shortly after taking off this

20   morning. Flight number 2234 . . ." James turned pale.

"My flight," he said out loud. "If I hadn't overslept, I'd have been on that plane."

A Oral questions

1 What was James's play about?
2 Did everyone expect it to be terribly successful?
3 Who bought it?
4 So what did they invite him to do?
5 Why didn't he wake up at 5.45?
6 Why did his alarm clock stop?
7 How did he discover what the time was?
8 What did he do when he found it was ten to nine?
9 What was the first item on the news?
10 Why did James turn pale?

IF I HADN'T OVERSLEPT, I'D HAVE BEEN ON THAT PLANE

B Look carefully at these *third conditional* situations arising from the story. Fill in the gaps with *would have* or *wouldn't have*.

1 If James hadn't written the play, the Americans . . . bought it.
2 If the Americans hadn't bought it, they . . . invited him to go to New York.
3 If they hadn't invited him to go to New York, he . . . booked a flight.
4 If he hadn't booked such an early flight, he . . . had to get up so early.
5 If he hadn't had to get up so early, he . . . needed to set the alarm.
6 If he hadn't forgotten to set the alarm, it . . . gone off.
7 If the mini-cab driver hadn't overslept, he . . . taken James to the airport.
8 If the mini-cab had taken James to the airport, he . . . checked in on time.
9 If he'd checked in on time, he . . . been on that plane.
10 If he'd been on the plane, he . . . been killed.

C Look at this conversation:

"I wouldn't have made it like that."
How . . . ?
"How would you have made it?"

*Reply to the following remarks with a **third conditional** question.*

1 I wouldn't have typed it like that.
   How . . . ?
2 You shouldn't have bought it there.
   Where . . . ?
3 That was a silly thing to do.
   What . . . ?
4 I wouldn't have paid as much as that.
   How much . . . ?
5 I wouldn't have told her about it.
   Why . . . ?
6 That was a stupid thing to say.
   What . . . ?
7 I wouldn't have gone there.
   Where . . . ?
8 I think you were silly to go by train.
   How . . . ?

9 I wouldn't have gone there on a Sunday.
   When . . . ?
10 I'd have bought it at Harrods.
   Why . . . ?

D Read Tom's story

"I was in love with a girl called Gloria. Eventually I asked her to marry me, but she refused. I was very upset and felt I needed a change, so I decided to go abroad for a short holiday. I chose Luzern as I had friends there.

"One day I went for a trip on the lake in a little pleasure boat. I was sitting on the deck, when a dark, pretty girl took the seat next to mine. I got into conversation with her, and she told me that she was Spanish, and that she was visiting Switzerland as the companion to an elderly lady from Argentina. She told me that she intended to come to England to learn English, so we exchanged addresses. Her name was Isabel.

"When I got home, I wrote to Isabel. She replied, and I found her an au pair job with an English family, not far from where I live, in Surrey. After I'd asked her several times, she agreed to go out with me. Three weeks ago we got married."

Note this pattern:

I was in love with Gloria/I asked her to marry me.
If I hadn't been in love with Gloria, I wouldn't have asked her to marry me.

Use the ideas below to make more sentences:

1 Gloria refused to marry me/I was upset
2 I was upset/I decided to go abroad for a holiday
3 I have friends in Luzern/I chose to go there
4 I was in Luzern/I decided to go for a trip on the lake
5 I decided to go for a trip on the lake/I met Isabel
6 The old lady from Argentina wanted to go to Switzerland/Isabel went there
7 We met on the boat/She gave me her address
8 She gave me her address/I wrote to her
9 She wrote to me/I found her the au pair job
10 I found her the au pair job/She came to England
11 I asked her several times to come out with me/She came out with me
12 She came out with me/We got married

UNIT 29   Third Conditional:

IF I HADN'T OVERSLEPT, I'D HAVE BEEN ON THAT PLANE

E   Idea for discussion

Consider Tom's story. If Isabel hadn't sat down beside him on the deck of the little pleasure boat, he would probably never have got into conversation with her, and they would never have seen one another again. That moment changed Tom's life.

Think of moments like this, and decisions you have made, perhaps, which have changed your life. Talk about them.

Note the forms of the THIRD CONDITIONAL:

STATEMENTS	If I'd (I had) seen the advertisement	I'd have (would have) applied for the job.

NEGATIVES	If I hadn't (had not) seen the advertisement	I wouldn't have (would not have) applied for the job.

QUESTIONS	Would you have applied for the job	if you'd (had) seen the advertisement?

and the **continuous** forms:

STATEMENTS	If the engine had been losing a lot of oil	I'd have noticed.

NEGATIVES	If the engine hadn't been making a funny noise	I wouldn't have noticed.

QUESTIONS	Would you have noticed	if the engine had been losing a lot of oil?

Special points to note

This is the tense we use when we are being 'wise after the event'.

"IF I HADN'T BEEN LATE, I WOULDN'T HAVE GOT THE SACK."

It is the tense we use when we are discussing things which might have happened in the past, but didn't. The big difference between this Conditional and the First and Second Conditionals is that the First and Second Conditionals refer to ideas that may still take place, while Third Conditional ideas never will.

"If the alarm had gone off, he'd have woken up." (but it didn't, and *he* didn't!)

In fact, of course, Third Conditional ideas are a combination of two tenses, the Past Perfect and the Third Conditional.

IF I HADN'T OVERSLEPT, I'D HAVE BEEN ON THAT PLANE

Mr Jones in the Magistrate's Court

Herbert Jones was a salesman. He had been stopped by the police and
accused of driving while under the influence of alcohol.

"Do you plead guilty or not guilty?"

"Not guilty Sir."

5   The policeman who had stopped Mr Jones was called to give evidence:
"I was on duty in Oxford Street on the afternoon of sixteenth May, when a
red Cortina overtook the police car at a speed considerably greater than the
forty-eight kph limit. I followed him down Oxford Street and signalled
him to stop. As soon as I put my head through his window, I smelt alcohol.

10   I asked the defendant if he had been drinking, and he replied: "Only a
couple of whiskies." I then asked him to take a test, which he did, and the
result was positive. I then asked him to accompany me to the police
station, where he was examined by a doctor and given a blood test. Again
the test was positive."

15   "Well, Mr Jones," the magistrate looked at the defendant, "is what the
constable says correct?"

"Yes Sir," said Mr Jones, "but if I lose my licence, I shall lose my job,
and I'm a married man with children. I only had two whiskies and a couple
of beers. I wasn't drunk."

20   "Very well," said the magistrate, "I find you guilty. I'm imposing a fine
of £25 and you are disqualified from driving for one year. I'm sorry about
the job, but you should have thought of that before you drank those
whiskies."

Mr Jones handed over his licence and left the court, looking a very
25 worried man. "If only I hadn't had that last whisky," he said to himself.

A Do this exercise. Be careful. Some of the questions are tricky.

1 Ask why the policeman stopped Mr Jones.
2 Answer the question.
3 Ask what crime Mr Jones was accused of.
4 Answer the question.
5 Ask why the policeman requested Mr Jones to take a breath test.
6 Answer the question.
7 What was the result?
8 What did the policeman then ask Mr Jones to do?
9 What happened at the police station?
10 How exactly was Mr Jones punished?

UNIT 29 Third Conditional:

IF I HADN'T OVERSLEPT, I'D HAVE BEEN ON THAT PLANE

B Look at this idea:

Mr Jones was driving too fast. The policeman stopped him. If he hadn't been driving too fast, the policeman wouldn't have stopped him.

*Use the situations below to make more **third conditional** sentences.*

1 The policeman was on duty on sixteenth May. He stopped Mr Jones.
2 The red Cortina overtook the police car. They signalled to the driver to stop.
3 The policeman signalled to Mr Jones to stop. He knew they wanted to speak to him.
4 Mr Jones had been drinking. The policeman smelt alcohol.
5 The policeman smelt alcohol. He asked Mr Jones if he'd been drinking.
6 The policeman thought Mr Jones had drunk a fair amount. He asked him to take a breath test.
7 The test was positive. The policeman asked Mr Jones to accompany him to the station.
8 The test was positive. They asked a doctor to come to the station.
9 The doctor was there. He gave Mr Jones a blood test.
10 Mr Jones was a married man. He was so worried about losing his job.
11 They took away his licence. He lost his job.
12 He drank that last whisky. He was over the limit.

C You will often want to say things like this:

"If I'd known it was going to be so cold, I'd have put on warmer clothes."

"If I'd known it was going to be so difficult to get spare parts, I wouldn't have bought it."

Look at the situations below and make similar sentences.

1 George and Tim went to a pop concert. The tickets cost £3.00 each. Tim said:

2 Daniel invited Roger to the party, but Roger got terribly drunk. Daniel said:
3 Susan and Mary went to a special exhibition of Greek Art at the Royal Academy. There was a terribly long queue waiting to get in. Mary said:
4 Tom and Jenny went shopping. Suddenly it started pouring with rain. Jenny didn't have her umbrella. She said:
5 Tony and David went to have tea in an old-fashioned tea shop. It looked very nice, but the service was very slow. There was a self-service café across the road. David said:
6 Louise agreed to go for a drive with Frank. But Frank drove terribly fast. Louise said:
7 Jenny and Susan went to a dance, and discovered that they were wearing identical blue dresses. Susan said:
8 Frank and Mike travelled back from Bournemouth along the M4 motorway. But there was a terrible lot of traffic. There is another road. Frank said:
9 Susan and Jenny decided to go to Brighton by train, instead of taking Susan's car. The train was dreadfully crowded. Susan said:
10 Mike and Richard decided to fly to Edinburgh, instead of going by train. When they saw the plane, they were shocked. It was terribly old. Richard said:

D Composition: A Moment which Changed My Life

Look again at Tom's story (exercise D in the first part of this unit), and write a story about yourself.

When you have written your story, look at it and see if you can make six **third conditional** sentences like this:

If I HADN'T GONE to the disco that night, I WOULDN'T HAVE MET Fred.

The Mad Tiler of Catford

Do you remember Uncle Podger, fixing the picture on the wall, in *Three Men in a Boat*?

Recently I moved into a new flat. The previous tenant was a man called Mr Baker. Privately we call him "The mad tiler of Catford", because
5 everywhere that tiles could be fixed, he fixed them; crazy rows of crooked tiles.

Mr Baker was do-it-yourself mad. He did his own plumbing – all the taps dripped, and all the joints leaked. He did his own electrical repairs – it was a miracle that the house never caught fire, and he made holes in the
10 walls. I don't know exactly what for, but whenever he needed one hole, he made three or four; and any wall space that was not covered over with tiles was decorated with wallpaper bearing a pattern of large, brightly coloured flowers. Purple and yellow were his favourite colours.

Unkind friends say I am an idle man, but I prefer to leave such jobs to
15 the expert. I had the tiles removed and replaced where necessary by a builder. I had the flat rewired by proper electricians, and I had the plumbing put in order by a real plumber.

What the builder and the electricians and the plumber said about Mr Baker's efforts was worth writing down and recording for posterity. But
20 unfortunately the language they used was not the sort of language that foreign students of English should learn!

Finally, when the builder and the electricians and the plumber had done their work, I got a young painter and decorator to paint all the walls white, and I had pale green carpets laid. My bank manager was very kind
25 and understanding, and my overdraft[1] should be cleared by the Christmas after next.

A Oral questions

1 In which book can you read about Uncle Podger?
2 What did the writer do recently?
3 Why did they call Mr Baker the "mad tiler of Catford"?
4 What was the result of Mr Baker's plumbing?
5 What might have happened as a result of Mr Baker's electrical repairs?
6 What was the wallpaper covered in?
7 What do unkind friends say about the writer?
8 What did the writer have done by a builder?
9 What did he have done by electricians?
10 What did he have done by a plumber?
11 What did he have done to the walls?
12 What did he have done to the floor?
13 Who was kind and understanding?
14 What did he allow the writer?

---

[1] overdraft: the bank has allowed him credit for a certain time

UNIT 30   To Have/Get Something Done

B Imagine that you visited the flat with the writer *before* he moved in. He said:

"We're going to have all those tiles removed."

Now use the notes below to say what other things he said he was planning to have done.

1 rewired
2 plumbing
3 walls
4 green carpets
5 double glazed
6 new ceiling/bedroom
7 central heating
8 new gas cooker/kitchen
9 new lighting/sitting-room
10 a shower

C Imagine that you have a lot of money! You go to look at an old farm that you are thinking of buying and turning into your new home.

Look at this idea:

"We can turn the stables into a garage."
"We can HAVE the stables TURNED INTO a garage."

Turn the following statements into have something done expressions.

1 We can make the kitchen bigger.
2 We can fix a new roof.
3 We can paint the outside white.

4 We can chop down the trees at the side of the house.
5 We can plant some apple trees at the back.
6 We can build a wall at the front, to make it more private.
7 We can make a tennis court over there.
8 We can plant peach trees along that wall.
9 We can build a swimming pool in that corner.
10 We can put in a telephone.

D Imagine you bought the farm and did all the things mentioned above. Two people pass by. One says:

"Oh, look! I think they've had the stables turned into a garage."

What did they say about all the other changes that had occurred?

E Idea for discussion.

In America rich people, usually women, but not always, spend huge sums of money having operations done, to make themselves look younger or more desirable.

They have facelifts, sticking-out ears "flattened", hair transplants, and the shape of their noses changed.

Discuss this idea:

All these operations are a ridiculous waste of money, and the surgeons concerned should be ashamed of themselves.

Note the forms of TO HAVE/GET SOMETHING DONE:

STATEMENTS	We're going to We'll We usually	have get	the car repaired at this garage.
	She	had got	her ears pierced* last week.

* ears pierced: holes made in them, so that she can wear earrings.

NEGATIVES	We aren't going to We won't We don't usually We didn't	have get	the car repaired at this garage.

QUESTIONS	Are you going to Will you Do you usually Did you	have get	your hair cut here?

Special points to note

You will find the HAVE/GET SOMETHING DONE construction useful whenever you wish to talk about something that you engage an EXPERT to do, instead of doing yourself.

Here are some more typical examples:

I'M GOING TO HAVE MY WATCH OVERHAULED.
I'VE HAD A TELEPHONE PUT IN.
GEORGE GOT THE RECORD PLAYER MENDED.
WHEN ARE YOU GOING TO GET THAT WINDOW
REPAIRED?
I DECIDED NOT TO HAVE THOSE PHOTOS ENLARGED.
I THINK WE'LL HAVE A NEW BATH FITTED.

Tim's Jaguar

Tim's a big, cheerful fellow, who lives two doors down the road from me.
He drives one of those little red post office vans that you see racing from
pillar-box to pillar-box, collecting the mail.

5 For a long time he's wanted one of those big Jaguars, the sort that
gangsters and wealthy bookmakers used to ride about in, the kind that
used to zoom past you, in the fast lane of the motorway, in the early sixties.

Now he's got one – a bargain too. It was stolen from outside a house in
Blackheath, one summer evening. The owner looked out of the window,
and saw it being driven away. He rang the police. There was a chase and
10 the Jaguar ended up in somebody's front garden, with a smashed wing.
The owner did all right out of the insurance, and sold it to Tim for £125.

He's had the brakes repaired, a new wing fitted, a reconditioned engine
put in, the old one was just about worn out, and finally he's had the car
resprayed black. Every Sunday morning, as I go to get the papers, I see
15 him, with a little smile on his face, polishing it lovingly.

A Do this exercise:

1 Describe Tim.
2 What does he do?
3 What sort of car has he wanted for a long time?
4 What sort of people used to buy them?

5   Why did the former owner of Tim's new car get a shock one summer evening?
6   What did he do?
7   What did a police car do?
8   What happened to the Jaguar?
9   Why was the owner prepared to sell it to Tim so cheap?
10   What did Tim do about the brakes?
11   What did he do about the damaged wing?
12   What did he do about the engine?
13   Why?
14   Ask what he had done to the outside.
15   Answer the question.

B   Look at this sentence:

"The brakes weren't working properly, so I had them repaired."

Use the ideas below to make similar sentences.

1   My watch wasn't going properly . . . (*overhaul*)
2   The photograph was very good . . . (*enlarge*)
3   My shoes had holes in them . . . (*repair*)
4   The car wasn't going well . . . (*service*)
5   The carpet was dirty . . . (*clean*)
6   My shirts were dirty . . . (*wash*)
7   The new speaker was faulty . . . (*exchange*)
8   The old apple tree was bearing no fruit . . . (*cut down*)

C   Look carefully at the following situations, and write one *have something done* sentence for each.

1   Mr Renton's watch hasn't been going well. He's taken it to a watchmaker, who has looked at it and given him a receipt.
2   Mr Kirk went on a fishing holiday in Scotland. He caught some fine trout and took them to the cook at the hotel. All the guests ate some of the trout that evening.
3   Mr Jones is in the shoe shop, holding an old pair of his shoes. The shoemaker has just quoted him £4 to have them repaired. Mr Jones is shaking his head.

4   Mrs Jones is in the hairdresser's. Her hair is going a little grey. The assistant is showing her the different colours that hair can be dyed.
5   Mr Frost read an article about the danger of driving on worn tyres. He's standing beside his car and the mechanic is looking very carefully at his tyres.
6   Mr Cobb is sitting in the barber's, waiting his turn. He has an interview tomorrow, and he wants to look smart.
7   Miss Potts is in the dentist's waiting-room. She has a back tooth that has been hurting for days.
8   Mrs Fox is in the cleaners waiting to be served. She has her husband's grey suit in her hand.

D   Composition

People always want what they haven't got.

Has it ever occurred to you that while fashionable African ladies are spending a lot of money having their hair straightened, their European sisters are doing precisely the opposite – having curls put in their hair . . .

Now you complete the composition.

Irregular Verbs

Here is a list of one hundred and one of the most useful irregular verbs. You will need to learn all of these. They are in groups to make it easier for you to learn them.

be — was — been
beat — beat — beaten
become — became — become
begin — began — begun
bend — bent — bent
bite — bit — bitten
bleed — bled — bled
blow — blew — blown
break — broke — broken
bring — brought — brought

build — built — built
burn — burnt — burnt
burst — burst — burst
buy — bought — bought
catch — caught — caught
choose — chose — chosen
come — came — come
creep — crept — crept
cut — cut — cut
deal — dealt — dealt

dig — dug — dug
do — did — done
draw — drew — drawn
drink — drank — drunk
drive — drove — driven
eat — ate — eaten
fall — fell — fallen
feed — fed — fed
feel — felt — felt
fight — fought — fought

find — found — found
flee — fled — fled
fly — flew — flown
forget — forgot — forgotten
freeze — froze — frozen
get — got — got
give — gave — given
go — went — gone
grow — grew — grown
hang — hung — hung
(hanged — hanged for people.)
hear — heard — heard

hide — hid — hidden
hit — hit — hit
hold — held — held
hurt — hurt — hurt
keep — kept — kept
know — knew — known
learn — learnt — learnt
leave — left — left
lend — lent — lent
let — let — let

lie — lay — lain
lose — lost — lost
make — made — made
mean — meant — meant
meet — met — met
pay — paid — paid
put — put — put
read — read — read
ride — rode — ridden
ring — rang — rung

rise — rose — risen
run — ran — run
see — saw — seen
sell — sold — sold
send — sent — sent
shake — shook — shaken
shine — shone — shone
shoot — shot — shot
show — showed — shown
shut — shut — shut

sing — sang — sung
sink — sank — sunk
sit — sat — sat
sleep — slept — slept
slide — slid — slid
smell — smelt — smelt
speak — spoke — spoken
speed — sped — sped
spend — spent — spent
spill — spilt — spilt

spit — spat — spat
spread — spread — spread
stand — stood — stood
steal — stole — stolen
stick — stuck — stuck
swear — swore — sworn
sweep — swept — swept
swim — swam — swum
swing — swung — swung
take — took — taken

teach — taught — taught
tell — told — told
think — thought — thought
throw — threw — thrown
understand — understood — understood
wake — woke — woken
wear — wore — worn
win — won — won
wind — wound — wound
write — wrote — written